PREPARE FOR
COUNCIL POWER
AND THE Dictatorship
OF THE
Proletariat

PREPARE FOR COUNCIL POWER AND THE Dictatorship OF THE Proletariat

GERALD MCISAAC

Printed in the United States of America

ISBN 978-1-957009-78-0 (sc)
ISBN 978-1-957009-79-7 (hc)
ISBN 978-1-957009-80-3 (e)

Library of Congress Control Number: 2022952123

History
2023.01.09

CONTENTS

CHAPTER 1

Abortion: The Issue That Is Dividing the Working Class

As the title suggests, the working people in North America, by whom I mean the working class, the proletariat, as well as the middle class, the petty bourgeois, are deeply divided, upon the issue of abortion. It is safe to say that almost everyone, among the working people, is either in favour of some form of legalized abortion, referred to as "pro choice", or dead set against legalized abortion, referred to as "pro life". Almost no one is indifferent, which is to say has no opinion, concerning the subject of abortion.

As an aside, I should mention that I dislike both terms, "pro life" and "pro choice", as the implication is that the two are diametrically opposed. They are not. Yet as the terms are deeply entrenched in popular usage, I have chosen to use those terms, at least for the purposes of this article. Further, I have chosen to refer to the monopoly capitalists, the billionaires, the members of a class referred to as the bourgeoisie, as simply capitalists. They should not be confused with the small business owners, the middle class, the petty bourgeois, as such are the friends and allies of the proletariat.

It is also safe to say that the capitalists are quite happy about this division, within the working class. This despite the fact that, as a class, they largely comprise some of the few people whom are indifferent on the subject of abortion. Hooray for any issue which divides the working class!

The more the working people are fighting among themselves, the better for the capitalists! After all, the capitalists are not entirely stupid. They are well aware that capitalists and workers are class enemies. A divided working class is a weak working class. The more the working class is divided, fighting among themselves, the better for the capitalist class. Divide and conquer!

As for those who think that I am overstating the situation, consider the opinion of Mao Tse Tung, a great revolutionary Marxist, the one who led the Chinese revolution to victory, in 1949.

As Mao stated, at the time of the Chinese revolution, it is of the *"first importance"*, to determine our friends and our enemies. That was as true then, as it is now. Rest assured, all members of the proletariat, as well as the most of the petty bourgeois, are friends, regardless of their personal views on abortion. Their common enemy is the capitalists, the bourgeoisie.

I should add that at the time of the Chinese revolution, the situation was quite complicated. There were various classes involved. These involved the proletariat, the peasants, the landlords, the middle class, the bourgeoisie, the intelligentsia, as well as the invading imperialists.

The current situation, at least here in North America, is no where near as complex. The capitalists have done a most impressive job of simplifying the class struggle! Most of the middle class, the small business owners, as well as the family farmers, the equivalent of the peasants, have been all but wiped out! Now it is us versus them, the working class against the capitalist class, the proletariat against the bourgeoise!

That being said, it is important to bear in mind that there was a reason the Chinese revolution of 1949 succeeded. As Mao stated, "the basic reason why all previous revolutionary struggles in China achieved so little was their failure to unite with *real friends,* in order to attack *real enemies* . . . we must pay attention to uniting with our real friends in order to attack our real enemies". (my italics)

I mention this as a means of stressing the importance of uniting with "real friends, in order to attack real enemies". Those who are pro life are not the enemy of those who are pro choice! We are all working people, either working class, proletarians, or middle class, petty bourgeois. We have a common enemy!

The alternative, that of fighting among ourselves, will give rise to the same result as that of all Chinese revolutionary struggles, prior to 1949. Basically nothing. In other words, as long as we are fighting among ourselves, we can expect to accomplish next to nothing.

Another great revolutionary leader, that of the great Lenin, also had a few words to say on the subject. Immediately after the successful socialist October Russian revolution of 1917, he wrote an article titled Left Wing Communism, An Infantile Disorder. He pointed out that capitalism, by its very nature, gives rise to a "large number of exceedingly motley types, intermediate between the proletarian and semi-proletarian", including the petty artisan and handicraft worker. He went on to say that the proletariat is also divided into "more developed and less developed strata", as well as those of "territorial origin, trade, sometimes according to religion, and so on". Now that is a rather accurate description of our current situation!

As passions are running so high, concerning the issue of abortion, may I suggest that all concerned "take a deep breath", sit down and try to gain some serenity. I much recommend this to that of "taking a valium"! Screaming at those who are of a different opinion than that of our own, is "counter productive", to state it politely. To phrase it in more popular, but perhaps more accurate terms, it is nothing other than "simple stupidity"!

With a little reflection, I think we can all agree that capitalism creates the conditions which give rise to "unwanted pregnancies". This is a polite way of saying that women who are raped, frequently do not want to give birth to the child of a rapist. Who can blame them? Of course, there are numerous other examples I could list.

With that in mind, may I suggest that we put aside our deep differences, some of which are based on religious beliefs, and focus on the best way to destroy the system that gives rise to wide spread instances of rape, sexual assault and child molestation, among other things. Of course I am referring to capitalism. The capitalists have to be overthrown, and that is a "tall order".

First and foremost, this requires a strong, united proletariat, in alliance with the middle class. If nothing else, everyone can agree that there is strength in numbers! This is not to imply that we must exchange hugs and kisses. That is not necessary. It simply means that we must respect each other, and that includes our different beliefs. Despite our differences, we are friends, all members of either the working class or the middle class, complete with a common enemy, the capitalist class.

Overthrowing capitalism is referred to as "getting to the root of the problem", and makes so much more sense than exchanging insults. After the revolution, after the capitalists are overthrown and crushed under the Dictatorship of the Proletariat, the conditions which give rise to the vast majority of unwanted pregnancies will be eliminated. At that point, those who are classified as "pro life" and those who are classified as "pro choice", can get together and resolve their differences. It is very likely that by then, it will amount to little more than a "tempest in a tea cup".

Without doubt, our class enemies will make every effort to continue to divide us. The last thing they want to see is a united proletariat! To that end, we can expect them to accuse us of hypocrisy! As they are the ultimate hypocrites, they take great delight in accusing others of their vices! They would much rather see us at each others throats!

It is certainly *not* hypocrisy to put aside our differences and unite against our common enemy! In fact, it is good common sense!

A fine example of this "common sense" happened many years ago, during the "Colonial Rebellion of the Seventeen Seventies", as the British refer to it, or the "Revolutionary War of Independence", as the Americans phrase it. It all depends on your view point!

During that Revolutionary War, various classes came together. The capitalists of the northern colonies united with the slave owners of the southern colonies. As well, the workers, small business owners, family farmers -peasants-, tradesmen, frontiersmen and in fact people from all walks of life, including former slaves, came together against their foreign rulers, the British nobility. Americans with deep differences came together, including those whom had every reason to hate each other, under far more difficult circumstances, and launched a successful revolution. They did it once, they can do it again!

In 1776, there were a considerable number of colonials who remained loyal to the "Crown", the British nobility. These were referred to as Tories. Most of them were reasonably wealthy, and correspond to the middle class intellectuals of today. The revolutionaries targeted them, publicly humiliated them, with the use of "tar and feathers". The middle class defenders of capitalism would do well to take note of the manner in which their Tory ancestors were treated!

As well, American diplomats appealed to the French nobility. Not that the French nobility was any different from the British nobility. The American colonials merely took advantage of the hostility between the two groups of nobility, and used it to their advantage.

I use these as mere examples of the different tactics which were used in this particular class struggle, that of the first American Revolutionary War. As is often the case, a straight forward assault, upon the ruling class, is nothing more than a suicide charge! Just as the American revolutionaries formed an alliance with the French nobility, to the benefit of the American revolution, so too we must form alliances. The point being that we must not only unite, but also attempt different tactics.

We want to get as many working people involved in the political struggle, against the capitalists, as possible. To this day, there are a great many working people, honest, hard working, law abiding citizens, who truly believe that their democratically elected leaders represent them. We must respect their beliefs. They deserve our utmost respect. They are going to have to learn, from their own experience, that the bourgeois politicians serve the capitalists. What better way to do this, than by electing some of their own, proletarian politicians, and sending them to Washington? After all, the most vocal supporters of capitalism tell us that if we do not like the system, we should "change it from within". Excellent idea!

As Lenin pointed out, "politics is a science and an art that does not fall from the skies or come gratis, and that, if it wants to overcome the bourgeoisie, the proletariat must train its *own* politicians, 'class politicians', of a kind in no way inferior to bourgeois politicians". (italics by Lenin)

For that reason, in previous writings, I have recommended that all Americans join the two mainstream political parties, as card carrying members. This may be against the "rules", but not the law, so feel free to be naughty. After all, it is the card carrying members of each party, who determine the candidates for each and every political office. If sufficient Americans join the two parties, then it is possible to flood Washington with "Leftist", proletarian politicians. These people can in turn support Senator Sanders and the members of The Squad. Democracy in action! Majority rule! Ha!

In such a case, the capitalists will not allow the working class to seize power, through "majority rule". They will be sure to make that abundantly clear! In that way, even the least advanced workers will learn, from experience, that the Communists are correct, that the capitalists have to be overthrown and crushed, under the Dictatorship of the Proletariat.

We can only stress the fact that the flooding of Washington with Leftist politicians will *not* result in political power being placed in the hands of the workers. It *will* serve to raise the level of awareness of the proletariat. Working people will learn, from their own experience, that democracy is *not* majority rule, but *class* rule! The capitalists are in charge, and they fully intend to remain in charge!

The idea of flooding Washington with Leftist politicians—"Bernie Bros"- is to serve the dual purpose of raising the level of awareness of the working class, as well as weakening Congress *from within*, in preparation for revolution and the subsequent Dictatorship of the Proletariat.

In addition, literature must be created, for the working class, written in terms which they can understand. The proletariat must be made aware that the word "proletariat" means worker. The Russian word "Soviet", merely means Council. The Soviet Union was, in English, the Council Union. Most working people are now becoming aware that workers Councils are taking shape all across North America. It is these Councils which must replace the current system of government, and that includes Congress. The Senate and House of Representatives must be dissolved, replaced by Councils of workers.

It is also a fact that working people need leaders. This is to say that a true political party must be created, one which serves the proletariat. Of course I am referring to a Communist Party, and there is an urgent need for such a Party. Yet the creation of such a Party is well beyond the ability of most working people. That is the point at which middle class intellectuals, those whom are aware of the revolutionary theories of Marx and Lenin, can prove to be most useful. Hopefully they too, can put aside their differences, including those concerning the subject of abortion, and cooperate.

It is Benjamin Franklin, the famous American revolutionary, who is credited with stating that "we can all hang together, or we can all hang separately". Well spoken! While that may not be literally true, the point is still valid. We can choose to fight among ourselves, concerning the issue of abortion, or we can unite to destroy capitalism, the very system which gives rise to unwanted pregnancies.

As I write this, demonstrations are taking place all across the country, demanding access to legalized abortion. Now if all that anger and enthusiasm could be directed against capitalism! That would make so much more sense!

These demonstrations are most gratifying, as it shows that working people, both proletarians and middle class people, are in motion, demanding change. Yet that state of mind, *by itself,* is not sufficient. In fact, it could well *harm* the revolutionary motion! That harm comes at the point where we are fighting *each other,* rather than the capitalists.

To repeat, it is the system of capitalism which gives rise to so many unwanted pregnancies -among a great many other things!- and until the capitalists are overthrown and crushed under the Dictatorship of the Proletariat, nothing of substance will change.

It is my most fervent desire that the people who are currently protesting, on both sides of the issue of abortion, should get together and agree to disagree. We are all working people, either proletarians or petty bourgeois, and have a common enemy. The capitalist class, the billionaires, the bourgeoisie. Divided, we fail. United, we succeed. Let us unite and overthrow the capitalists! May the banners of the protesters read:

Workers of the World, Unite!
Dictatorship of the Proletariat!

CHAPTER 2

The Difficulty In Maintaining State Power After The Revolution

Jan 15, 2022

INTRODUCTION

The current revolutionary motion is not limited to America. It is raging in capitalist countries around the world. In fact, this is similar to the years immediately following the successful socialist Russian October Revolution of 1917.

At that time, the most advanced strata of the proletariat, in the capitalist countries, had embraced the concept of Soviet Power, in that Soviet means Council. They had also embraced the Dictatorship of the Proletariat, according to Lenin. For that reason, he was of the opinion that it was essential to prepare the most advanced workers for revolution. The reason for that is quite simple. After the revolution, workers with very little training, or even no training at all, will be placed in positions of authority. Any training they receive now, will prove to be most valuable.

The big difference now, is that the most advanced workers of the world have not embraced the concept of Soviet (Council) Power, or of the Dictatorship of the Proletariat.

Yet the revolution could break out any day, as no revolution is "made to order". At that time, the existing state apparatus will be destroyed, and replaced with a new working class state apparatus, in the form of the Dictatorship of the Proletariat. Certain advanced workers will be placed in key positions of authority. Now it is imperative to raise their class consciousness, and prepare them for the approaching revolution.

Yet it is one thing for the proletariat to seize state power, it is something else entirely to hang onto that power. Classes will continue to exist, after the revolution, which is precisely the reason for the necessity of the Dictatorship of the Proletariat. The capitalist class will have to be crushed.

The experiences of previous, proletarian revolutions, has had mixed results. In each case, at some point after the workers seized power, the capitalists were able to return to power. It is the purpose of this article to determine those mistakes, so that we can avoid repeating them. At the same time, we have to take into account our current state of preparation.

With that in mind, consider the fact that it is significant that Lenin placed the recognition of Soviet Power on the same level as that of recognition of the Dictatorship of the Proletariat.

The key to maintaining state power, under the Dictatorship of the Proletariat, lies with both the Communist Party and, Soviet (Council) Power. In the words of Lenin, "Only the Communist Party . . . is capable of leading the proletariat in a final, most ruthless and decisive struggle against all the forces of capitalism. On the other hand, it is only under the leadership of such a Party that the proletariat is capable of displaying the full might of its revolutionary onslaught, and of overcoming the inevitable apathy and occasional resistance of that small minority, the labour aristocracy, who have been corrupted by capitalism, the old trade union and cooperative leaders . . . it is only after they have found an opportunity of organizing in their Soviets (Councils) in a really free way . . . that the masses, the toilers and exploited as a body, can display . . . all the initiative and energy of tens of millions of people who have been crushed by capitalism . . . It is only in the Soviets (Councils) that the exploited masses really begin to learn -not in books, but from their own practical experience, the work of socialist construction, of creating a new social discipline and a free union of workers."

It is also significant that at present, most working people have no idea of the meaning of the term "Soviet Power". For that matter, the term "Dictatorship of the Proletariat" is mere "Greek". That is certainly not acceptable. It has to be changed, and quickly.

It is up to class conscious people, those who are aware of the revolutionary theories of Marx and Lenin, to raise the level of awareness of the proletariat. Of necessity, most of these people are middle class, or at least have a middle class background.

It is entirely possible, that as the American proletariat becomes ever more class conscious, they will start to refer to these Councils as Soviets. That remains to be seen, and is entirely up to the workers. For the purposes of this article, I will refer to them as Councils.

The raising of the level of awareness of the working class is a "tall order", but not as difficult as it once was. The fact is that most working people are literate, and most of the advanced workers own a digital device, of one sort or another. That is important, as those are precisely the workers upon whom we are most focused. After all, it is the more advanced workers who lead, while the less advanced follow.

The capitalists have very thoughtfully provided us with a valuable tool, in the form of the internet. It is truly a marvel of modern technology. The least we can do is express our gratitude, our appreciation, by using this tool against them. God knows that they deserve it!

Councils, Also Known As Soviets

Even though most Americans have no idea of the meaning of the word Soviet, the fact remains that these Soviets, or Councils, are currently being created.

These Councils, to use the English expression, are formed as communities of workers come together, as a result of extreme pressure, especially at a time of revolutionary motion. These communities of workers then proceed to elect leaders, members of a Council. This can be compared to the creation of trade unions. There is an instinctive awareness that there is strength in numbers.

The Councils then attempt to improve the living standards within the community, to enact certain reforms. Under capitalism, this is supremely difficult, but not impossible, especially at a time when the situation is revolutionary. As Lenin phrased it, "symptomatic of any genuine revolution is a rapid, ten fold and even hundred fold increase in the size of the working and oppressed masses – hitherto apathetic – who are capable of waging the political struggle".

This "pressure from below", as the journalists describe it, often results in reforms, however paltry, especially during times of revolutionary motion. In this way, the working people learn that the capitalists are not "all powerful", that they can be beaten. This serves to empower the workers, builds up their self confidence, and encourages them to undertake even greater challenges. As Marx phrased it, "Reforms serve to strengthen and further the revolutionary motion".

With that in mind, the experience of the city of Seattle is instructive. In that case, a section of the city, an area referred to as Capitol Hill, attempted to break away and form an independent community. As people lived and worked together, assisting and caring for one another, it was nothing other than a Commune. It was also self governing, with the elected leaders forming a Council. The local police precinct was even forced to close. This was first referred to as the Capitol Hill Organized Protest. Then, in a touching display of optimism, the Council decided to be Autonomous. So the name was changed to the Capitol Hill Autonomous Zone.

Naturally, the government regarded this as nothing less than a threat to their authority. After all, state power can be in the hands of one class or another, but not both. As the Zone was in the hands of the working class, they wasted no time in attempting to destroy it. At the same time, they tried to crush the Council.

Perhaps the government agents thought, in the simplicity of their souls, that by crushing the Capitol Hill Autonomous Zone, that would be the end of all Councils. Such is hardly the case! Instead, it has served to educate other Councils. There are no more illusions. People are now aware that "half measures get you nowhere". Now it is "all in", a "war to the finish".

It is clear that revolutionary Councils are being created, all across America, and probably in other countries as well, as was predicted by Lenin. Of necessity, these Councils are keeping a "low profile", arming, training and equipping workers, in preparation for the Revolution. The Insurrection is critical, at which time the government will be overthrown, and the element of surprise is of great importance.

These Soviets, or Councils, had humble beginnings. They first appeared in 1905 Russia, at the time of the first Russian Russian. As

Lenin stated, "The Soviet form of organization came into being in the spontaneous development of the struggle".

It was spontaneous, if for no other reason than that, in Russia, at that time, almost all of the Social Democrats, as the Marxists of the day referred to themselves, had been first thrown into prison, and then were either killed or exiled. Lenin had been exiled.

In Russia, as the 1905 Revolution was crushed, so too were the Soviets, the Councils. There followed several years of reaction, before the revolutionary motion picked up again. At that time, the Soviets reappeared, only this time, far more numerous, far more powerful. But then the Second Russian Revolution was in full swing.

These Councils are not to be under estimated.

After the first February-March revolution of 1917, in Russia, in which the Czar was overthrown, a "democratic republic" was established. This is to say that with the Czar out of the way, the capitalists were able to seize state power.

Yet, the power of the capitalists was being challenged, by the power of the Soviets (Councils). These proletarian Councils represent state power!

As Engels stated, "periods occur when the warring classes are so nearly balanced that the state power, ostensibly appearing as a mediator, acquires for a moment, a certain independence in relation to both". It was Lenin who pointed out that immediately following that the February revolution, under the reign of the Kerensky government, the power of the Soviets (Councils) was very nearly the equal of the capitalists!

Incidentally, present day historians are fond of mentioning that the Russian government agents, under Karensky, should have "arrested"

Lenin, as soon as he stepped off the train, upon his return to Saint Petersburg, in April of 1917. To such dedicated flunkies of the capitalists, I can only respond that no doubt, the "thought crossed their minds". Yet the power of the working people, as expressed in the Soviets (Councils), prevented them from so doing. (I placed the word Council after Soviet in order to stress the importance)

After the Socialist October Revolution of 1917, the working class seized power and established the Dictatorship of the Proletariat. The leaders of that Revolution were well aware that it was necessary to organize the working people, both workers and peasants. As Lenin stated in March, 1919, "We remembered very well the part the Soviets has played in 1905, and revived them as the most suitable means of uniting the working people in their struggle against the exploiters . . . We see that the Soviets are gaining popularity in the west, and that the fight for them is going on not only in Europe, but also in America. Soviet type Councils are being set up everywhere, and sooner or later they will take power into their own hands. The present situation in America, where such Soviets (Councils) are being set up, is extremely interesting . . . This form has superseded all other forms of proletarian organization."

As the Councils are the "most suitable means of uniting the working people in their struggle against the exploiters", it is up to Communists to offer them our complete and undivided support. Without doubt, it is just a matter of time before they "take power into their own hands".

As an aside, it is interesting to note that America has a proud history of Councils, a history which has been carefully concealed, by the capitalists.

Lenin then went on to explain the "Essence of the Dictatorship of the Proletariat and of Soviet Power":

"The victory of socialism . . . over capitalism requires that the proletariat . . . shall accomplish the following three tasks. First— overthrow the exploiters, and first and foremost the bourgeoisie . . . utterly rout them; crush their resistance; absolutely preclude any attempt on their part to restore the yoke of capital and wage-slavery. Second - win over and bring under the leadership of the Communist Party, the revolutionary vanguard of the proletariat, not only the entire proletariat, or its vast majority, but all who labour and are exploited by capital; educate, organize, train and discipline them in the actual course of a supremely bold and ruthlessly firm struggle against the capitalists; wrest this vast majority of the population in all the capitalist countries from the dependence on the bourgeoisie; imbue it, through its own practical experience, with confidence in the leading role of the proletariat and of its revolutionary struggle. Third - neutralize, or render harmless the inevitable vacillation between the bourgeoisie and the proletariat, between the bourgeois and Soviet Power, to be seen in the class of petty proprietors in agriculture and commerce - a class which is still fairly numerous in nearly all advanced countries, although comprising only a minority of the population - as well as in the stratum of intellectuals, salary earners, etc., which corresponds to this class".

Clearly, this is well beyond the ability of Councils, which tend to be local in character. It serves to point out the necessity of a true Communist Party, one which recognizes Council Power and the Dictatorship of the Proletariat.

Yet, as many of the members of these Councils are intellectuals, many of them have a middle class background. As such, they are aware of the revolutionary theories of Marx and Lenin. As that is the case, they are *duty bound* to go beyond the training of workers, and to prepare for the revolution. They have to take the next step, that of taking part in the creation of a truly revolutionary, Communist Party, one which endorses Soviet Power and the Dictatorship of the Proletariat.

THE NECESSITY OF A TRUE
COMMUNIST PARTY

The current political situation is similar to the situation in Europe, 1918. Writing in October of that year, Lenin addressed the fact that there were no Communist Parties in Europe: "Europe's greatest misfortune and danger is that it has *no* revolutionary party. It has parties of traitors . . . and of servile souls like Kautsky. But it has no revolutionary party. Of course, a mighty, popular revolutionary movement may rectify this deficiency, but it is nevertheless a serious misfortune and a grave danger." (italics by Lenin)

Yet Lenin did more than point out that "serious misfortune" and "grave danger" of "*no* revolutionary party". He went on to give direction to the true revolutionaries: "That is why we must do our utmost to expose renegades like Kautsky, thereby supporting the revolutionary *groups* of genuine internationalist workers, who are found in *all* countries. The proletariat will very soon turn away from the traitors and renegades and follow these groups, drawing and training leaders from their midst. No wonder the bourgeoisie of all countries are howling about "world Bolshevism". World Bolshevism will conquer world bourgeoisie". (italics by Lenin. At that time, Communism was referred to as Bolshevism)

Even though this was written a hundred years ago, it is -unfortunately- still relevant. Lenin refers to Kautsky as a "renegade", because that is precisely the case. At one time, Kautsky was a fine Marxist, a leading theoretician. The work which Kautsky did, in his days as a Marxist, was superb. That cannot be denied. Nor can it be denied that at some point, under severe pressure from the capitalists, Kautsky "turned his coat". He became a "renegade", a "Benedict Arnold", a traitor to Marxism, a traitor to the proletariat.

During the time that Kautsky was a Marxist, he did a fine job, in the service of the working people. After he "turned his coat", became a renegade, he also did a fine job, but in the service of the bourgeoisie! His distortions of the revolutionary theories of Marx, are a marvel! To this day, the capitalists sing his praises! It is no wonder that Lenin referred to Kautsky as his "bitterest enemy!". He went on to say that "there is no point in fighting with Kautsky. It is simply a matter of exposing his apostasy!" This is to say that Kautsky was simply a traitor, and his treachery had to be documented. That is as true today, as at the time it was first written!

I mention this, because it is of the utmost importance. As the revolutionary motion gains strength, as ever more working people are swept up in the movement, becoming politically active, they will spontaneously gravitate towards socialism. The expression "Dictatorship of the Proletariat" will soon become common place. The social chauvinists are sure to respond by referring workers to the revisionist works of Kautsky. We, in turn, must respond by referring workers to the book by Lenin, The Proletarian Revolution and the Renegade Kautsky, in which Lenin exposes Kautsky, as the traitor to socialism, that he was. Now to proceed.

Lenin went on to state that once the Communist Party is formed, it is faced with the task of "intensifying the preparation of the proletariat". This includes making the working people aware of the true meaning of the terms Soviet (Council) Power, and that of the Dictatorship of the Proletariat.

At the moment, a "mighty, popular revolutionary movement" is sweeping the country. No doubt a great many workers will initially be attracted to the political parties which claim to be socialist, the "traitors and renegades" to socialism, but then become disillusioned and "walk away", in turn joining the "revolutionary groups of international workers", those "who are found in all countries". These groups will be "drawing and training leaders from their midst". These groups are referred to as Councils.

It is up to the leaders of these Councils to form a true Communist Party. Of necessity, the membership of the Party must be exclusive, limited to those who are true Marxist-Leninists. The most advanced workers, those who have been trained by the Councils, qualify for membership.

Lenin made clear the importance of Councils, which he of course referred to as Soviets: "It is only in the Soviets that the exploited masses really begin to learn -not in books, but from their own practical experience -the work of socialist construction, of creating a new social discipline and a free union of free workers."

Yet the capitalists are determined to not allow the existence of Councils, as they see these as a threat to their authority. The experience of the Seattle Autonomous Zone, which was brutally crushed, proves this, beyond any doubt. These Councils can only thrive under socialism. That requires a revolution, and the subsequent Dictatorship of the Proletariat.

In turn, this can be accomplished only through the leadership of the Communist Party. Only such a Communist Party is able to organize a proper Insurrection, overthrow the capitalists, smash the existing state machine, and utterly crush their resistance, through the Dictatorship of the Proletariat. Equally without doubt, many will point out that it is not fair to place this burden on the shoulders of a few intellectuals. True. It is not fair. Life is not fair. It is what it is. There are times when it is necessary to take a stand. Now is one of those times.

There is a reason that the revolutionary theories of Marx and Lenin are known, almost exclusively, to middle class people, petty bourgeois.

It is only in universities that these theories are "taught", or to state it more accurately, it is only in universities that these revolutionary theories are "distorted". As university training is limited, almost entirely, to the bourgeois, very few working class people are aware of these theories.

Yet as so many middle class intellectuals have attended university, they are aware of those revolutionary theories. Which is not to say that all intellectuals embrace those theories! In fact, a great many of them refuse to even acknowledge those theories, unless it is to distort them. This distortion of the theories of Marx and Lenin, is referred to as "revisionist". The social chauvinists go to considerable length to revise those revolutionary theories, in order to make them acceptable to their Lords and Masters, the capitalists, the billionaires. Revolution is not acceptable to the bourgeoisie. The Dictatorship of the Proletariat is absolutely not acceptable! Social reform is quite acceptable. For that reason, the social chauvinists want to divert the revolutionary motion onto some harmless path of social reform. All of the currently existing "Leftist" political parties, or at least those which refer to themselves as Marxists, are simply revisionists.

It may be objected that the true "upper class" people, the bourgeoisie, the billionaires, also generally receive a university education. True. Yet their money allows them to buy any university degree their little hearts desire! They may not even attend any classes! As a result, they may, or may not, be aware of those revolutionary theories. Either way, such details are a matter of complete indifference to them.

The point being that most intellectuals are middle class, or at least have a middle class background. For many years, such people tended to remain silent, as it was in their best interests to do so. After all, even the accusation of being a Communist could result in career suicide!

Yet lately there has been a "bit of a change", to use a British understatement. That has come in the form of the Corona Virus, which has now been raging for two years. During that time, numerous restrictions have been put into place, in terms of gatherings and travel. This has resulted in the closure of countless small businesses. The owners, members of the middle class, petty bourgeois, are being ruined. As well, various intellectuals and salaried employees are also losing their jobs. All are joining the ranks of the proletariat. They bring with them their knowledge of the revolutionary theories of Marx and Lenin.

This has resulted in a growing awareness among the middle class, as well as the intellectuals and the salaried employees, that the current political situation is unacceptable. The capitalists are forcing this awareness upon those people! You could even say that they are doing our work for us! Awfully sweet of them! We really should send them a thank you card! They are doing such a fine job of digging their own graves!

Of course, monopoly capitalism leads to the destruction of all small businesses. As the monopolies become ever stronger, ever more complete, all small businesses are eventually ruined. The Virus has merely served to "accelerate the course of world history". Ever more small businesses are being ruined, as a result of the Virus, ever more quickly. As well, the revolutionary motion of the proletariat is also increasing.

As a result of this, we are now blessed with a great many intellectuals, newly minted members of the proletariat. It is up to those intellectuals, either current or former members of the middle class, to put their training and experience to good use. Of course I am referring to the formation of a true Communist Party. Such a Party is needed to lead the working class

No doubt the government is quite well aware that all of the existing Leftist political parties are of no great concern, as all are merely calling for reforms, of one sort or another. That is not a threat to the capitalists. A true Communist Party, one which is based upon the revolutionary theories of Marx and Lenin, is very much a threat. For that reason, they are monitoring various people, those whom they consider to be a threat. Also, certain government agencies have programmed their computers to tune into the phone calls of people, to "flag" certain words, and then record the conversations. Feel free to determine those words, and avoid them. As well, there is something referred to as the "dark net", which can be used, instead of a phone.

The act of creating a Communist Party will no doubt attract the attention of various government agencies, if they become aware of it, so it is best to use reasonable precautions. There is no longer any need to gather in person, as Lenin did, when he created the Russian League of Struggle For the Emancipation of the Working Class. He was also promptly arrested. Try to avoid that, if for no other reason than that those Communists who are in prison, are of limited usefulness. Besides, there is no shortage of Communist martyrs!

My advice, for these freshly minted intellectual Marxists, is to not only take part in creating a Communist Party, but to change your behaviour. Our goal is to raise the level of awareness of the working class, to prepare them, or at least the most advanced workers, for Council Power and the Dictatorship of the Proletariat. After the revolution, these workers will be placed in key positions of authority.

With that in mind, feel free to "lose the jargon", or as the workers put it, "quit speaking High English!". Get in the habit of speaking in a more popular manner, so that working people can understand you. All working people have their pride, and do not want to "look stupid". For that reason, they tend to remain silent, when they hear things they do not understand, and even go to the length of avoiding intellectuals. That is the last thing we want!

Under no circumstances resort to vulgarity! We want to raise the level of awareness of the workers, not to personally sink to a lower level. Feel free to use metaphors, even sports metaphors. Bear in mind that I am well aware of your attitude towards professional sports, as no doubt it matches my own. Put aside those personal prejudices and focus on the bigger picture.

When referring to workers, avoid the use of the word "backward". They may get the idea that they are being called "stupid" or "ignorant". It is not their fault that their vocabulary is limited! Instead, use such terms as "advanced" and "less advanced". Bear in mind that with the revolutionary motion growing and spreading, ever more workers are being picked up, joining the movement, blurring the distinction between the advanced and the less advanced.

Also, avoid such words as "masses", when referring to the members of the public, as people tend to find it impersonal, even offensive. Instead, use expressions such as "common people", or the "rank and file". Perhaps "blue collar" is acceptable, assuming workers know the meaning of the term.

The word "opportunist" is also common place among Marxists, but most workers are not aware of the meaning. Such terms as "without principle" is an acceptable alternative. Feel free to call a factory a factory, and not a "point of production". The same applies to railroads and shipping lines. And by all means, avoid "i.e." Almost no worker knows what it means!

The expression "third world country" should also be avoided. It was an expression dreamed up by the social chauvinists, in order to revise the revolutionary theories of Marx and Lenin. Bear in mind that

Lenin referred to Russia as a "petty bourgeois" country, as at the time of the revolution, the majority of people were peasants. Perhaps the term "under developed" country is more acceptable, and a term working people can understand. It is also a fact that Lenin referred to highly industrialized countries as "cultured" countries, not "first world".

It is unfortunate that the expression "third world country" is now in popular use, so perhaps if you must use it, feel free to qualify the remark by an initial "so called".

The expression "Dictatorship of the Proletariat" will soon become very popular. To most working people, this is "Greek", a bit of "High English". Yet it is one of the expressions the working class is going to have to master, as it is so extremely important.

Do not "water it down"! Do not refer to this as the "rule of the working class", because it is not! As Lenin stated, "Dictatorship is rule based directly upon force and unrestricted by any laws. The revolutionary Dictatorship of the Proletariat is rule won and maintained by the use of violence, by the Proletariat, against the bourgeoisie, rule that is unrestricted by any laws."

The point must be driven home, to all workers, that after the revolution, under the Dictatorship of the Proletariat, the capitalists, the billionaires, will not be protected by any laws! They will not be allowed to hide behind a team of lawyers! There will be no lawyers! The capitalists will have no rights! The Proletariat will crush all capitalists, as well as those who challenge the authority of the working class. That includes thieves and killers, rapists and child molesters. Those who do not contribute to society, choose to live as thieves, do not "pull their own weight", will soon wish they had! The workers will see to that!

Then again, it is a fact that working people are going to have to become familiar with certain scientifically correct words, such as "proletarian and bourgeois". In such cases, when speaking to more advanced workers, feel free to use the scientific term, followed by the common term. When speaking to the less advanced workers, there is no point in using scientific terms. Such workers tend to not pay any great attention to intellectuals. It is the advanced workers to whom they listen.

This may all sound very simple, as it is, but not necessarily easy. Old habits are so hard to break! Yet they must be broken, as there is no other way to gain the trust and respect of the workers.

NAME OF THE PARTY

As the title of this article suggests, my main concern is with maintaining political power, after the revolution. It is one thing to seize political power, to establish the Dictatorship of the Proletariat, and it is quite another to hold onto that power. Of course, I am referring to the Paris Commune, the Soviet Union and Communist China. At one time, they were socialist. But then the capitalists were able to return to power. Clearly, certain mistakes were made, by the leaders. More on that subject, later on in this article.

The fact is that I am quite confident that the next American revolution will take place rather soon, and further, that it will be successful. By that I mean that the working class will rise up, overthrow the existing government, smash the state apparatus which is currently being used to crush the working class, and set up a new working class state apparatus, in the form of the Dictatorship of the Proletariat. This has been done before, as previously mentioned. And yet, the capitalists managed to return to power. We have to learn from the mistakes of previous revolutionaries, in order to avoid repeating them.

I am also confident that a proper American Communist Party is taking shape. By "proper" I mean one that is based on the revolutionary theories of Marx and Lenin. That certainly includes the Dictatorship of the Proletariat, the "touchstone" of a true Marxist, according to Lenin.

Incidentally, I managed to get my hands on an English translation of an article, written by Engels, in 1891, of his Introduction to an article written by Karl Marx, titled The Civil War in France. In that article, he refers to the "Dictatorship of the Proletariat". Capitalization by Engels. As he felt that the theory was so important, he used those capital letters, and I will follow his example.

We have got to distinguish ourselves from the other "Leftist" political parties, those which are social chauvinists! If there is one thing that unites the chauvinists, perhaps the only thing, it is their opposition to the Dictatorship of the Proletariat! As it is the worst night mare of the bourgeoisie, the chauvinists want nothing to do with it! For that reason, may I suggest that the name of the Party become, American Communist Party, Dictatorship of the Proletariat. ACP,DP.

No doubt, some may object that in March of 1918, Lenin approved the name change of the Party, from the Russian Social Democratic Labour Party of Bolsheviks, to the Russian Communist Party (Bolsheviks), or RCP(B). That is true. Yet the only reason he placed the word Bolsheviks in brackets, was because it was so meaningless. In fact, it means majority in Russian, as opposed to Menshevik, which means minority.

The term Dictatorship of the Proletariat expresses a fundamental tenet of Marxism. It is anything but meaningless, and should not be placed in brackets, but instead be separated by a comma.

LESSONS FROM PREVIOUS REVOLUTIONS:
THE PARIS COMMUNE

As Lenin put it, "A mistake remains a mistake, so it is necessary to criticize it, and fight for its rectification".

With that in mind, let us consider the first successful attempt, by the proletariat, to seize political power. Of course I am referring to the Paris Commune of 1871, France. The Commune was brief, surviving a mere few weeks, before it was crushed, with the utmost brutality. In fact, it resulted in a "blood bath of defenceless prisoners". I mention this for the sake of working people, who are interested in such details.

One of the favourite responses of the social chauvinists is to point out that Marx, who was living in Britain at the time, foresaw that the rebellion was approaching, considered that it was "desperate folly", and in the fall of 1870, advised against it. True. Yet the rebellion was forced upon the workers, and they rose to the occasion. As Marx put it, the heroic Communards "stormed the very gates of heaven"!

Of course there is a reason that the social chauvinists mention this. They are trying to forestall the American revolution! They would have us believe that the approaching socialist revolution is also "desperate folly"! They will also quite cheerfully point out that the American workers are not prepared to seize political power! That too is true! The capitalists are constantly bombarding the working class with distortions and outright lies, as a means of maintaining control, as part of their method of rule. They are making every effort to ensure that the workers are never prepared for the Dictatorship of the Proletariat! It is up to us to educate workers, to prepare the working class for Council Power and the Dictatorship of the Proletariat! That is our *duty*!

It is instructive to note that at the time of the Paris Commune, there was a gentleman by the name of Kugelmann, who was also of the opinion that the workers of Paris should never have revolted. Marx wrote to him and expressed his opinion, in terms which left no room for any misunderstanding: *"World history would indeed be very easy to make, if the struggle were taken up only on condition of infallibly favourable chances"*. (italics by Lenin)

The point is that the working class is in motion. Revolutionary motion. I refer to this as an Act of God. It is just a matter of time, and probably a short time, before the workers rise up and "storm the gates of heaven", so to speak. In other words, take part in a full blown Revolution. This Insurrection, if successful, will result in the downfall of the current government, and the destruction of the current state apparatus, that which is being used to crush the working class. The only question being: What will replace the current government?

For the benefit of the advanced workers, those who are just now becoming politically active, I will mention that "mass movements" happen. Common people rise up spontaneously, as for example in America, 1776, or in France several years later. Frequently, these movements have no leaders, although leaders do emerge. The point being that the people who are in motion, frequently by the millions, are not aware of that which they are doing. In fact, they are making history! This is called being spontaneous. Yet it in no way changes the fact- and it is a fundamental tenet of Marxism- that "the masses are the makers of history!"

As previously mentioned -and I say it again by way of emphasis- the social chauvinists are well aware of this! Their plan is merely to take over the existing state apparatus, at the time of the revolution, and set themselves up as the new rulers! The last thing they want to see, is the destruction of the state apparatus! Perish forbid! There is a method to their madness!

Now to return to the popular Insurrection, which is bound to happen. If the uprising is spontaneous, the chances of success are not that great. After all, the capitalists have had a great many years to prepare for such an assault. They are not entirely stupid!

By contrast, if the Insurrection is well planned, as was the Insurrection in Russia, on November 7, (new style calendar), or October 25, (old style calendar), 1917, then it has every chance of being successful. The events of January 6, 2021, in the capitol of Washington, have served to reveal the weakness of the capitol! And that, in turn, serves to reveal the importance of a Communist Party! Only such a Party can organize a proper Insurrection!

To return to the lessons of the Paris Commune. As brief as it was, it provided Marx with the information he needed, and he subjected the Commune to a careful analysis in his book, The Civil War In France. (Bear in mind that the leaders of the Commune were Prondhonists and Blanquists. Neither paid any attention to the advice of Marx)

The Commune did away with the standing army, and armed the whole people. It proclaimed the separation of church and state, abolished state payments to religious bodies, made popular education purely secular. In addition, night work in bakeries was forbidden, and the system of fines was abolished. A decree was issued that all factories and work shops, which had been abandoned or shut down by their owners, were to be turned over to associations of workers, and were to resume production. A second decree was issued, to the effect that the salaries of all administration and government officials, regardless of rank, could not exceed the normal wages of a worker. Further, such officials were subject to recall at any time. Excellent! Yet the Commune made a number of serious mistakes.

Immediately after the workers of Paris rose up and seized power, the former government fled to the neighbouring city of Versailles. The workers of the Commune, the Communards, failed to attack them! No doubt their attitude was one of "live and let live". A huge mistake! As Lenin phrased it, "In rising against the old regime, the proletariat undertook two tasks -one of them national and the other of a class character- the liberation of France from the German invasion and the socialist emancipation of the workers from capitalism. This union of two tasks forms a unique feature of the Commune". The workers, Communards, were "blinded by patriotic illusions". Lenin went on to say: "Combining contradictory tasks -patriotism and socialism- was the fatal mistake of the French socialists . . . the task of the proletariat was to fight for the socialist emancipation of labour from the yoke of the bourgeoisie".

It is safe to say that the Communards went "half way". There is some truth to the expression that "half measures get you nowhere". The banks were not taken over. The workers attempted to "exert moral influence" on the government which had fled to Versailles. Fat chance! As a result of these "half measures", the government in Versailles was able to gather enough forces to crush the Commune. A fine example of half measures getting somewhere- into an early grave!

The point must be driven home that the working class, the proletariat, must be focused. It must be focused on destroying their class enemies, the capitalists, the bourgeoisie. There must be no distractions!

There is one other comment by Marx, which I consider to be of vital importance, especially as it is frequently overlooked: "Having once got rid of the standing army and the police, the physical force elements of the old government, the Commune was anxious to break the *spiritual force of repression*, the "parson power"". (my italics)

It is clear that Marx was careful to distinguish between the "physical force elements of the old government", which is quite obvious, and the "spiritual force of repression", which is far less obvious. Both are part of the state apparatus, which is used to crush the working class, and as such, has to be destroyed. Yet all too often, the spiritual forces of repression are overlooked. We will return to this later.

Perhaps the most important lesson learned from the Commune, is that the proletariat "cannot simply lay hold of the existing state apparatus and use it for their own purposes"! Instead, the state apparatus, which has been set up by the capitalists, in order to crush and exploit the working class, must be "smashed, destroyed", according to Marx. A separate state apparatus must then be set up, in order to "crush the desperate and determined resistance of the bourgeoisie", as they "try to restore their paradise lost", as per Lenin! This new state apparatus is referred to as the Dictatorship of the Proletariat.

RUSSIAN OCTOBER REVOLUTION

The next revolution on our hit parade, is the socialist, October Revolution of 1917, Russia, so called because it took place on October 25, old style calendar, or November 7, new style calendar. It was successful, against all the odds, because it was led by Lenin, and Lenin was careful to follow all the guide lines of Marx.

All historians, including the most devoted servants of the bourgeoisie, are agreed that Lenin had his hands full! At that time, Russia was an underdeveloped country. It was huge, over three times the size of the continental United States, sparsely populated, but with the majority of the people, three quarters in fact, being peasants. Yet there were other classes in the country. These included the nobility, the landlords, the middle class small business owners, or petty bourgeois, the monopoly capitalists, or bourgeoisie, the peasants, whom were in turn divided into poor, middle and rich, and of course the workers, or proletarians.

Naturally, this gave rise to various political parties, each of which claimed to represent the interests of one particular class. Each party had to be taken into account. As well, the country was at war with Germany and the Central Powers. Yet the revolution succeeded!

I mention this for the sake of those who are skeptical, who think that the American revolution cannot possibly succeed, as the monopoly capitalists, the billionaires, are too powerful, and the working class in not prepared. Such is not the case! In 1917 Russia, under far more difficult circumstances, a socialist revolution succeeded, but only because of the leadership of the Communist Party, with Lenin at the head. He relied upon the working class, the proletariat, as well as the vast majority of poor peasants.

As long as we have the backing of the "common people", other wise known as the "members of the public", the "rank and file", which is to say the "working people", the poor peasants -farmers- and the proletariat, then we can work miracles! It worked in Russia, it will work here!

The difference is that the current political situation is much simpler, as the capitalists have thoughtfully clarified matters. On the one hand, we have the capitalists, the billionaires, the bourgeoisie, and on the other hand, we have the workers, the proletariat. We have no nobility, and only the remnants of other classes, the peasantry (farmers) and the middle class. Now it is "us" against "them". This can only work to our advantage, because, as Lenin pointed out, "in every capitalist society, the only *decisive* forces are the proletariat and the bourgeoisie". (italics by Lenin) We fully intend to teach the bourgeoisie the meaning of the word "decisive"!

After the death of Lenin, in 1924, it was Stalin who became the leader of the Soviet Union. He in turn carried to completion the work which Lenin had started. A most backward, under developed, predominantly peasant country, was transformed into a highly industrialized socialist republic. As a result of two Five Year Plans-planned production- the Soviet Union was able to accomplish, in ten years, that which it had taken the capitalist countries, one hundred years! At the time of the revolution, Russia was one hundred years behind America. Yet at the end of the second five year plan, the country had caught up!

This enabled the Soviet Union to withstand the Nazi invasion of 1941, that which the Soviets referred to as the Great Patriotic War. This victory would have been inconceivable without socialist construction in the Soviet Union.

Yet after the death of Stalin, the Russian capitalists were able to return to power. This prompted the Chinese Communists to conduct a criticism of Stalin.

In particular, Chairman Mao tse-tung, on behalf of the Communist Party of China, CPC, wrote an open letter to the Communist Party of the Soviet Union, CPSU, in which Stalin was defended. This letter is contained within the Selected Works of Mao, and titled On the Question of Stalin. As it is so vitally important, I have decided to quote it at length. A great revolutionary leader has been terribly slandered, and continues to be slandered. As a matter of principle, he must be defended.

It should be mentioned that, due to the diligent efforts of the bourgeois censures, it is most difficult to obtain a copy of this letter. But as Mao wrote:

"The CPC -Communist Party of China-has always held that when Comrade Khruschev completely negated Stalin, on the pretext of 'combatting the personality cult', he was quite wrong and had ulterior motives . . . this . . . violates Lenin's integral teaching on the interrelationship of leaders, Party, class and masses, and undermines the Communist principle of democratic centralism . . .

"The great Soviet Union was the first state of the Dictatorship of the Proletariat. In the beginning, the foremost leader of the Party and Government in this state was Lenin. After Lenin's death, it was Stalin . . .

"After Lenin's death, Stalin became not only the leader of the Party and government of the Soviet Union, but the acknowledged leader of the international Communist movement as well . . .

"The CPC has consistently maintained that the question of how to evaluate Stalin and what attitude to take towards him is not just one of appraising Stalin himself; more important, it is a question of how to sum up the historical experience of the Dictatorship of the Proletariat and of the International Communist movement since Lenin's death . . .

"The CPC insists on an overall, objective and scientific analysis of Stalin's merits and demerits, by the method of historical materialism and the presentation of history as it actually occurred, and has opposed the subjective, crude and complete negation of Stalin by the method of historical idealism and the willful distortion and alteration of history . . .

"Stalin did commit errors, which had their ideological as well as social and historical roots. It is necessary to criticize the errors Stalin actually committed, not those groundlessly attributed to him, and to do so from a correct stand, and with correct methods. But we have consistently opposed improper criticism of Stalin, made from a wrong stand and wrong methods . . .

"Stalin fought czarism and propagated Marxism during Lenin's lifetime; after he became a member of the Central Committee of the Bolshevik Party, headed by Lenin, he took part in the struggle to pave the way for the 1917 Revolution; after the October Revolution he fought to defend the fruits of the proletarian revolution . . .

"Stalin led the CPSU -Communist Party of the Soviet Union- and the Soviet people, after Lenin's death, in resolutely fighting both internal and external foes, and in safe guarding and consolidating the first socialist state in the world . . .

"Stalin led the CPSU in upholding the line of socialist industrialization and agricultural collectivization and in achieving great successes in socialist transformation and socialist construction . . .

"Stalin led the CPSU, the Soviet people, and the Soviet army in an arduous and bitter struggle, to the great victory of the anti fascist war . . .

"Stalin defended and developed Marxism-Leninism in the fight against various kinds of opportunism, against the enemies of Leninism, the Trotskyites, Zinovienites, Bukharinites, and other bourgeois agents . . .

"Stalin made an indelible contribution to the International Communist movement, in a number of theoretical writings, which are immortal Marxist-Leninist works . . .

"Stalin led the Soviet Party and Government in pursuing a foreign policy which on the whole was in keeping with proletarian internationalism and in greatly assisting the revolutionary struggles of all peoples, including the Chinese people . . .

"Stalin stood in the forefront of the tide of history, guiding the struggle, and was an irreconcilable enemy of the imperialists and all reactionaries . . .

"Stalin's activities were intimately bound up with the struggles of the great CPSU and the great Soviet people, and inseperable from the revolutionary struggles of the people of the whole world . . .

"Stalin's life was that of a great Marxist-Leninist, a great proletarian revolutionary . . .

"It is true that while he performed meritorious deeds for the Soviet people and the International Communist movement, Stalin, a great Marxist-Leninist and proletarian revolutionary, also made certain mistakes. Some were errors of principle, and some errors were made in the course of practical work; some could have been avoided, and some were scarcely avoidable at a time when the Dictatorship of the Proletariat had no precedent to go by . . .

"In his way of thinking, Stalin departed from dialectical materialism and fell into metaphysics and subjectivism on certain questions and consequently he was sometimes divorced from reality and from the masses. In struggles inside as well as outside the Party, on certain occasions and on certain questions, he confused two types of contradictions, which are different in nature, contradictions between ourselves and the enemy, and contradictions among the people, and also confused the different methods used in handling them. In the work led by Stalin in suppressing the counter revolutionaries, many of the counter revolutionaries deserving punishment were duly punished, but at the same time, there were innocent people who were wrongly convicted; and in 1937 and 1938 there occurred the error of enlarging the scope of the suppression of counter revolutionaries. In the matter of Party and government organizations, he did not fully apply proletarian democratic centralism and, to some extent, violated it. In handling relations with fraternal Parties and countries, he made some mistakes. He also gave some bad counsel in the international Communist movement. These mistakes caused some losses to the Soviet Union and the International Communist movement . . .

"Stalin's merits and mistakes are matters of historical, objective reality. A comparison of the two shows that his merits outweighed his faults. He was primarily correct, and his faults were secondary. In summing up Stalin's thinking, and his work in their totality, surely every honest Communist with a respect for history will first observe what was primarily in Stalin. Therefore, when Stalin's errors are being correctly appraised, criticized and overcome, it is necessary to safe guard what was primary in Stalin's life, to safe guard Marxism-Leninism, which he defended and developed . . .

"It would be beneficial if the errors of Stalin, which are only secondary, are taken as historical lessons, so that the Communists of the Soviet Union and other countries might take warning and avoid repeating those errors, or commit fewer errors. Both positive and negative historical lessons are beneficial to all Communists, providing they are drawn correctly and conform with, but do not distort historical facts . . ."

The article goes on to point out that Lenin considered people such as August Bebel and Rosa Luxemburg to be great proletarian revolutionaries, despite their mistakes. As Lenin phrased it, the proper approach is not to conceal those mistakes, but to learn "how to avoid them and live up to the more rigorous requirements of revolutionary Marxism".

Mao went on to say: "The leaders of the CPSU have accused the CPU of 'defending Stalin'. Yes, we do defend Stalin. When Khruschev distorts history and completely negates Stalin, naturally we have the inescapable duty to come forward and defend him, in the interests of the International Communist movement.

"In defending Stalin, the CPC defends it's correct side, defends the glorious history of struggle of the first state of the Dictatorship of the Proletariat, which was created by the October Revolution; it defends the glorious history of struggle of the CPSU; it defends the prestige of the International Communist movement, among working people through out the world. In brief, it defends the theory and practice of Marxism-Leninism. It is not only the Chinese Communists who are doing this; all Communists devoted to Marxism-Leninism, all staunch revolutionaries and all fair minded people have been doing the same thing.

"While defending Stalin, we do not defend his mistakes. Long ago, the Chinese Communists had first hand experience of some of his mistakes. Of the erroneous "Left" and Right opportunist lines which emerged in the Chinese Communist Party at one time or another. Some arose under the influence of certain mistakes of Stalin's, in so far as their international sources were concerned. In the late twenties, the thirties and the early and middle forties, the Chinese Marxist-Leninists, represented by Comrades Mao tse-tung and Lin shou-chi, resisted the influence of Stalin's mistakes; they gradually overcame the erroneous lines of "Left" and Right opportunism, and finally led the Chinese Revolution to final victory.

"But since some of the wrong ideas put forward by Stalin were accepted and applied by certain Chinese comrades, we Chinese should bear the responsibility. In its struggle against "Left" and Right opportunism, therefore, our Party criticized only its erring comrades, and never put the blame on Stalin. The purpose of our criticism was to distinguish between right and wrong, learn the appropriate lessons and advance the revolutionary cause. We merely asked the erring comrades that they should correct their mistakes. If they failed to do so, we waited until they were gradually awakened by their own practical experience, provided they did not organize secret groups for clandestine and disruptive activities. Our method was the proper method of inter Party criticism and self criticism; we started from the desire for unity and arrived at a new unity on a new basis through criticism and struggle, and the good results were achieved. We held that these were contradictions among the people, and not between the enemy and ourselves, and that therefore we should use the above method . . ."

A great revolutionary has been slandered, and continues to be slandered. We will do our best to correct that attack by the capitalists. The fact remains that the capitalists have managed to restore capitalism in Russia, using as an excuse, the mistakes made by Stalin. We are going to have to avoid those mistakes.

CHINESE GREAT PROLETARIAN CULTURAL REVOLUTION

Yet there can be no doubt that the response of the Chinese Communists, to the return to power by the Russian capitalists, was to launch the Great Proletarian Cultural Revolution. This revolution was truly magnificent, so that countless people rose up and attacked their class enemies, the capitalists, the professional people, those who were working in the field of culture. The police were not allowed to interfere, except in the case of murder, arson or rape. Without doubt, the common people received valuable training, in the class struggle. Yet upon the death of Mao, the capitalists were able to return to power. So what went wrong?

Perhaps we should face the fact that the Cultural Revolution was just that. Cultural. It was not Scientific. I use that word in the loosest possible sense, to include medical and educational. True, the Cultural Revolution touched upon acupuncture, and in fact there were significant advances made in that field. Yet that was an exception.

Without doubt, the capitalists were hiding in various fields of culture. The Cultural Revolution did a fine job of rooting them out! Yet the capitalists were also hiding in various fields of science! They remained hidden, biding their time. Upon the death of Mao, they emerged and managed to seize political power.

This brings me to my previous statement, to the effect that Marx referred to the *"spiritual force of repression"*. He made it clear that such a spiritual force was every bit as much a part of the state apparatus, as was the "police and standing army, the physical force elements of the old government". As such, both the physical and the spiritual, have to be destroyed. Was the spiritual force of repression destroyed in China?

There are various spiritual forces. In the case of the Paris Commune, Marx referred to the "parson power", the spiritual force of the clergy. Other spiritual forces include that of the mobsters, the landlords and the professional people, which includes the intellectuals and scientists. Common people have every reason to be terrified of the mobsters and the landlords. Yet the spiritual power of the professional people, which I refer to as "Professor Power", is more subtle.

Without doubt, the spiritual power of the landlords, in China, was broken. Mao made this quite clear in his excellent article, Report On An Investigation Of The Peasant Movement In Hunan. Lessons from this article can be applied to the approaching American Revolution.

One of the tactics the peasants used, to great effect, involved the use of a "spear corps". These spears were simple long poles, with metal blades on the end. Very simple and equally effective! The mere sight of a bunch of people, armed with spears, terrified their class enemies!

As that is the case, may I suggest that those same weapons be used, here in America. Numerous Councils have been formed, and they are currently arming, equipping and training workers. That equipment includes shields, night sticks, helmets, bullet proof vests and paint balls. They are also being trained in the use of firearms. Simple pipe wrenches can be used to open the fire hydrants, in order to reduce the water pressure, so as to neutralize the water cannons. Slings are also very handy, with projectiles of marbles, as a means of dealing with the "cavalry", the "cowboys" mounted on horses.

As spears proved to be so effective in China, no doubt they will also serve to create a lasting impression here in America, especially in regard to the "riot squad". One of the favourite tactics of the government forces, is to "lock shields" and advance towards peaceful protesters. They refer to this as "crowd control". Yet if that same "crowd" is armed with spears, they will no doubt have second thoughts on the matter. It is also a fact that should projectiles of marbles, launched from slings, fail to have the desired effect on horses, then rest assured, no horse will charge into a wall of spears.

But now to return to the Chinese Peasant Revolution:

As Mao phrased it, "The main targets of attack by the peasants are the local tyrants, the evil gentry and the lawless landlords, but *in passing* (my italics) they also hit out against patriarchal ideas and institutions, against the corrupt officials in the cities and against bad practices in the rural areas . . . the privileges which the feudal landlords enjoyed for thousands of years are being shattered to pieces. Every bit of the dignity and prestige built up by the landlords is being swept into the dust".

That which he mentioned "in passing" is critical. It suggests that he underestimated the importance of smashing the spiritual forces of repression. This helps to explain the fact that the Cultural Revolution was almost entirely limited to culture. It barely touched on science. This was due to the fact that the spiritual power of the professional people, those working in various fields of science, the "Professor Power", was not broken.

The "institutions" to which Mao referred, are part of the "physical force elements of repression". As they are part of the state apparatus, the peasants were absolutely correct in destroying them. They were also correct in attacking, or "hit out", against "patriarchal ideas" and "bad practices". That is part of the "spiritual force of repression" which also had to be destroyed. The peasants trusted their class instincts, and acted correctly! The "spiritual force of the landlords" was smashed!

As the power of the peasant associations grew, the "top local tyrants and evil gentry" made themselves scarce. They ran to the towns and cities.

Here in America, we have Councils being created. As yet, they are rather weak, but as they grow stronger, and exert ever more influence, we can expect the mobsters, as well as the "rich and powerful", to grab as much money as they can get their greedy little paws on, and head for "parts unknown".

In China, the peasant movement caused quite an uproar. In fact, the "gentry" found this to be appalling! Even the most progressive, true revolutionaries, began to use the word "terrible". Mind you, the most advanced revolutionaries qualified that statement by adding that "it is inevitable in a revolution". No one could deny that it was terrible! Yet all were mistaken!

As Mao pointed out, the peasant movement amounted to the "forces of rural democracy", rising up against the "forces of rural feudalism". These forces were the "corner stone of imperialism, warlordism and corrupt officialdom". They had to be destroyed, and they were destroyed. The only correct revolutionary response is to say, "that is fine!"

AMERICAN REVOLUTION

We can expect a similar response here in America, at the time when the working people, led by the Councils, and hopefully a Communist Party, rises up to challenge the authority of the capitalists, the mobsters, and even the scientists. No doubt, the journalists, the loyal lapdogs of the capitalists, will be roused to a frenzy of "righteous indignation"! Let them rage! They too will become a target of the revolution!

We can also expect the more "moderates", the "centrists", to take their own stand. They will play the role of the "elder statesman", the "profound philosopher", whose "words of wisdom drip from their lips like drops of precious pearls". In fact, they are nothing other than loyal servants of the capitalists! Bleeding hearts, one and all! Quite predictable!

These centrists will state that the movement is "going too far", that people certainly have "legitimate grievances", but that "everyone should respect the law". Those who break the law "should be brought to justice". Nonsense!

It never crosses the mind of these simple souls that a great many people are about to be "brought to justice"! Proletarian justice! A Revolution is not a tea party! It is first and foremost an Insurrection, an act of violence by which one class overthrows another! It is not to be confused with needle point! The capitalists, the billionaires, have to be overthrown! That requires something more than a stern lecture! At the same time, the mobsters, thieves, sex offenders and assorted lowlife, can and will be held accountable!

These people, the class enemies of the proletariat, will not be allowed to hide behind high priced lawyers! The days of "pleading the fifth" will soon be over! Instead, they will have to answer to "the people", the same people they have crushed and exploited for years! And make no mistake, the people keep track! They know precisely the book makers, the drug dealers, the thieves, the killers, the rapists and child molesters! The people will soon decide those who deserve the most severe punishment, and those who will receive less severe punishment.

It is noteworthy that at one point, Lenin was asked, by a corespondent, a question concerning war criminals. His response was instructive, in that his recommendation was to "educate them to useful labour and make them break with the shameful, base bloody role of exploiters and instigators of wars for the partition of colonies. War will then soon become absolutely impossible". Re-education through labour!

Among those who will receive leniency, are the professional people, the scientists, teachers, professors and such. Those are the people who are insisting, to this day, that dinosaurs are extinct, that the mega fauna are extinct, that people are responsible for climate change, in the form of global warming, that all sightings of UFO's are mere hocus pocus, that all sightings of Sasquatch are the product of overly active imaginations, that Ogopogo and the Loch Ness monster are fairy tales, and so on and so forth. Nonsense! The list is endless. In fact, the science and history books are filled with countless distortions and out right lies. These people will be held to account, but not to the extent of the mobsters, the sex offenders and the capitalists. Yet their spiritual power will be broken.

For the moment, the professional people are able to exercise a certain spiritual power over the common people, which I refer to as "Professor Power". It is part of the state apparatus, that which is used to crush the working people, and must be destroyed.

As for those who may suggest that this smacks of terror, I can only respond that you are so right. Bear in mind that there is a big difference between committing acts of terror on innocent citizens, such as the events of "nine eleven", and terrorizing the capitalists and lowlifes. The fact is that terror is required to overthrow the class enemies of the proletariat, to crush their resistance. As Mao put it, "Proper limits have to be exceeded in order to right a wrong, or else the wrong cannot be righted". This is to say that during a Revolution, the normal rules of polite, proper etiquette, do not apply!

We can expect the loudest opposition to be raised by the most patriotic citizens, the middle class, the petty bourgeois. As Lenin pointed out, these people, "owing to their economic position, are more patriotic than the bourgeoisie or the proletariat."

A sizeable portion of the petty bourgeois consists of the mobsters, those who are in the "business" of separating honest people from their money. That makes them middle class, petty bourgeois. They tend to diversify, rather than focus on any one field of endeavour, so that they are less effected by economic downturns. Indeed, they generally are involved in a wide range of businesses, which include dope dealing, boot legging, drug running, theft, gambling, prostitution, extortion, gun running, kidnapping and "human trafficking", which is to say the slave trade. They tend to be even more patriotic than most petty bourgeois, with good reason. After all, they will be the first to point out that nowhere else in the world, is it "so easy to make a dishonest buck"! The Constitution grants them rights, unmatched in any other parts of the world! All sex offenders are also of that opinion! They have every reason to be patriotic, to oppose the Revolution!

For our part, we can only do our best, to make sure that their worst nightmares come to pass! Perhaps the sex offenders, those who take great delight in abusing women and children, in private of course, should be allowed to spend a little more "quality time" with those ladies. One good turn deserves another! May I suggest placing those lowlifes in a room with all of their victims, or the mothers of the children, with whom they had such a great time, and then giving them a little privacy. Under the Dictatorship of the Proletariat, there is no statute of limitations!

At the time of the Chinese Revolution, during the uprising of the peasants, the ultimate punishment, that of execution, was rare, but it did happen. As Mao put it, "in the interests of eradicating the remaining evils of feudalism . . . the only effective way of suppressing the reactionaries is to execute at least a few in each county, who are guilty of the most heinous crimes".

Naturally, we are not cursed with the "remaining evils of feudalism", as the capitalists have eradicated that filth, for their own reasons, many years ago. Yet there is no shortage of reactionaries in the country! All too many of them have committed the most heinous crimes! No doubt a few of them will be executed, as a means of suppressing all other reactionaries. The workers will have a difficult time, trying to decide the chosen few! There are so many who deserve the death penalty! The competition is fierce! Yet once people are dead, they can no longer be the slightest bit useful. So the death penalty must be used sparingly. The remaining reactionaries must be sentenced to a life of manual labour, in remote locations, so that escape is out of the question. In that manner, even the reactionaries can do their part in building socialism!

Those who are guilty of less serious crimes can be sentenced to a term of labour, to be determined by the workers, involved in building socialism. Certainly our railroads have to be repaired and rebuilt. A great deal of work must be done in the country side. Our agricultural base needs a great deal of work, as does our woodlands. Countless areas which have been polluted by the capitalists, must be cleaned up. Who better to clean up the mess, than the people who made the mess?

LESSONS TO BE LEARNED

In conclusion, we can say that the heroic Communards of Paris did not smash the existing state apparatus, and further, that they tried to do two things at once. To build socialism, while remaining loyal to their country. A fatal mistake!

In the Soviet Union, Stalin made mistakes, which the capitalists seized upon. Then again, it was up to his closest advisors, the Members of the Central Committee, to offer him advice. We can say that they were negligent in their duty. After all, we are all human, so that we all make mistakes.

In Communist China, the spiritual power of the scientists, the "Professor Power", was not crushed. All such spiritual power, which is part of the state apparatus, and used to crush the working people, must be destroyed.

I submit that these are the lessons of previous revolutions. We must be sure to *not* commit those same mistakes.

CHAPTER 3

Political Platform For a True Canadian Communist Party

<u>Mar 21, 2022</u>

The revolutionary motion in Canada is growing ever more intense. There is an urgent need for a true Communist Party, one which is based on the revolutionary theories of Marx and Lenin. For that reason, I suggest the name include the demand for the Dictatorship of the Proletariat, as that is the "touchstone" of a true Marxist, according to Lenin. In this way, we can distinguish ourselves from the social chauvinists, those who are socialist in words, chauvinist in deeds. Such people want no part of the Dictatorship of the Proletariat.

With that in mind, I suggest the name of the Party be that of the Canadian Communist Party, Dictatorship of the Proletariat, CCP,DP.

As for the political platform, I can suggest the following list of demands:

1.) Canada must separate from Britain, no longer recognize the Queen as the head of state, and declare Canada to be a republic.

2.) Quebec is to be recognized as a separate country.

3.) Canada must withdraw from NATO.

4.) Abolish the Canadian Senate.

5.) Declare the national debt to be null and void.

6.) Open the borders to all refugees.

7.) The class consciousness of all working people must be raised.

8.) All prisons, including those referred to as "correctional institutions", should be closed.

9.) The death penalty should be applied only as a last resort.

10.) All government officials are to work at the wages of workers, and are subject to recall at any time.

11.) All large scale capitalist enterprises, which include but are not limited to the banks, factories, mills, mines, railroads, airlines and communications networks, are to become the property of the state.

12.) The middle class people, the petty bourgeois, are to be respected. They are the natural and desirable allies of the proletariat. Their property is to remain in their hands.

A little explanation is in order.

As Canada has not embraced militarism, and does not have a considerable bureaucracy, it is similar to Great Britain of 1871. At that time, Marx was of the opinion that a revolution was possible without the condition of first destroying the "ready made state machinery". For that reason, it is possible to "buy out" the capitalists. A team of professional negotiators should be assigned this task.

Each and every member of the Senate has been appointed by the Prime Minister. None of them has ever been elected. For that reason, the Senate should be abolished.

Canada must become a socialist republic, with power vested in the working class, the proletariat, and that power will be exercised under the Dictatorship of the Proletariat.

The precise form that this Dictatorship will take, is in the shape of Councils, or Soviets, as that is the Russian translation of the word. Lenin referred to these Soviets as "mass organizations", to include only the workers, no capitalists. After the Russian Revolution of October, 1917, he stated that "these Soviets wield all state power". He went on to say that "Soviet power must necessarily, inevitably, and in the not distant future, triumph all over the world".

For that reason, the various Councils, or Soviets (as yet we have no way of knowing which word will soon be used) must be enlarged, encouraged and strengthened. They have recently appeared, quite spontaneously, and as yet are rather weak, but are destined to "triumph all over the world".

As yet, the proletariat is not aware of itself as a class, complete with its own class interests. The more advanced workers should be encouraged to read the Essential Works of Lenin, including State and Revolution, Imperialism, the Highest Stage of Capitalism, and What Is To Be Done? More popular literature must be made available for the workers who are less advanced.

People who are guilty of serious crimes should be given the opportunity to perform useful, productive work, in the interests of contributing to society, and as a means of redeeming themselves.

Those who are considered to be a threat to society, such as sex offenders – rapists and "pedophiles", child molesters, – as well as "human traffickers" -slave traders-, are to also be isolated, perhaps in the Arctic, so that there is no chance that any of them can escape and once again prey upon people.

Those who are determined to overthrow the Dictatorship of the Proletariat, as a means of restoring capitalism, are to be considered political prisoners. They must be not only isolated, but also denied any contact with the outside world. As they are the leaders of the capitalists, the bourgeoisie, we can expect them to make every effort to cause trouble.

The courts must be abolished and replaced by a panel of working people. This is precisely what happened in the Paris Commune of 1871. As Marx stated, "The judicial functionaries were to be divested of their sham independence . . . Like the rest of the public servants, magistrates and judges were to be elective, responsible and revocable".

It must be emphasized to these judicial people that the death penalty must be administered only as an absolute last resort. Those who are dead can be of absolutely no use.

Student loans are to be considered part of the national debt, and cancelled. Education is to be free to all.

CHAPTER 4

Concerning the Necessity of Smashing the Existing State Apparatus

Dec 6, 2021

It is a basic tenet of Marxism, that immediately after the "Insurrection", the existing state apparatus must be smashed, and replaced with a different state apparatus, in the form of the Dictatorship of the Proletariat. Why is that? Further, how is it that the "social chauvinists" are so dead set opposed to this?

As I am writing this article for the benefit of those who are just now becoming politically active, it is first necessary to explain a few technical terms. We can start with the term "social chauvinist", which is to say a person who is "socialist in words, chauvinists in deeds".

Such a person claims to be a Marxist, but denies the necessity of smashing the existing state apparatus, and then replacing it with a different state apparatus, in the form of the Dictatorship of the Proletariat. Such people are also referred to as "revisionists", which is to say that they are determined to revise the revolutionary theories of Marx and Lenin. The revisionists would have us believe that those two great revolutionaries were nothing more than gifted reformers!

We must stress that these "social chauvinists", otherwise known as Marxist revisionists, are not to be confused with those who consider themselves to be Social Democrats or Democratic Socialists or just plain Socialists. We have no quarrel with such people, as they are the natural and desirable allies of the working class, the proletariat. They are our brothers and sisters, our comrades. Our goal is to unite with such people, in their struggle for reforms and general improvements in the living and working standard of the proletariat.

On the other hand, the revisionists, those who claim to be Marxists, but seek to revise the revolutionary theories of Marx and Lenin, to transform those revolutionary theories into a liberal program of democratic reform, are nothing other than agents of the capitalists, the billionaires, the bourgeoisie. As they are devoted servants of the billionaires, they are the enemies of the proletariat. Their goal is to divert the revolutionary motion onto some harmless path of social reform. For that reason, we must have nothing to do with them.

This brings me to the term "Insurrection", which is referred to as the rather short interval of time in which the classes in revolt, in our case the proletariat, rises up and attempts to overthrow the government which is crushing it.

In the case of a spontaneous uprising, the chances of the Insurrection being successful are not that great. Yet if the Insurrection is well planned and coordinated, with the key bridges, highways, water ways, tunnels, railroads and communications networks shut down, then it has every chance of success.

A very clear cut example of this is provided by the Russian Revolution of November 7 (new style calendar), 1917. On that day, the Russian government, which served the capitalists, and was led by the allegedly "socialist" minister Kerensky, was overthrown. But then the Insurrection was well planned and executed.

As the Insurrection was led by Lenin, the first order of business was to smash the existing state apparatus, and replace it with a new state apparatus, with the goal of crushing the capitalists, in their frenzied attempts to restore their "paradise lost". This new state apparatus is referred to as the Dictatorship of the Proletariat.

In modern terms, our existing state apparatus includes the presidency and his Cabinet, among other things. The members of the Cabinet are perhaps the ultimate bureaucrats, not elected but with great power. As well, there are numerous people who are placed in charge of various government agencies, all appointed by the president. These government postings are "political plums", rewards to the "party faithful" for their years of faithful service. All such agencies have been established with the express purpose of crushing the working class. As that is the case, they must be destroyed.

Other institutions have also been set up, in order to keep the "lower classes" in their "proper place". The prisons have proven to be quite useful, to the point of being most profitable. It was simply a matter of changing the name to "correctional facility", and handing them over to the capitalists. The idea is that the inmates are to be "corrected", shown the error of their ways, so that they can be sent back into society as proud, tax paying, law abiding citizens. Fat chance!

In fact, these criminals are provided with free room and board, clothing, recreation, entertainment, medical, dental, vision, hearing and professional councillors. All at tax payer expense! They also receive a valuable education in a life of crime! The life long inmates teach them the finer points of banditry! Not that it matters to the capitalists, because the more people who are in prison, the higher the profit!

These, among many others, are parts of the "state apparatus" that has to be smashed. It has been set up by the tiny minority of capitalists, in order to crush the vast majority of working people. So how is it that the social chauvinists are so dead set opposed to their destruction? Because they have their own agenda!

The social chauvinists, the revisionists, tend to be well educated. As such, they are supremely well aware of the revolutionary theories of Marx and Lenin. Yet there is a big difference between being aware of those theories and applying them! They know the revolution is about to happen, and have plans for this. Those plans do not involve smashing the state apparatus! On the contrary, at the time of the Insurrection, they plan to take control of the existing state apparatus, and set themselves up as the new rulers!

Lenin made that quite clear in his book, State and Revolution. It was written in the spring and summer of 1917, in preparation for the approaching socialist Russian Revolution. As that is the case, it is of the utmost importance, just as relevant today, as it was then.

He explained that the first attempt of workers, to establish their own government, did not take place until the spring of 1871. At that time, the workers in Paris, France, revolted and established the Paris Commune. It was only in existence for a few weeks, quickly crushed by the capitalists, yet provided Marx with the information he needed. The lessons, provided by the Paris Commune, were so important, that he and Engels decided that it was necessary to correct the Communist Manifesto. As they phrased it, "One thing especially was proven by the Commune, viz., *that the working class cannot simply lay hold of the ready made state machine and wield it for its own purposes*". Marx went on to stress the importance of *smashing* the existing state machine.

The workers who took part in the Paris Commune tried to take over the existing state machine, and use it for their own purposes. That was a huge mistake, as they effectively set themselves up as the new rulers. For that reason, Marx stressed the importance of destroying the existing state machine.

That mistake is of particular importance now, as the American empire is set to break apart, just as the Russian empire broke apart in 1917. Just as numerous socialist republics declared independence from Russia, so too, several American republics will soon follow suit.

The fact is that no less than three separate republics have already taken shape, within the borders of the continental United States. This includes seven states on the east coast, seven states in the industrial heart land of the midwest, and three states on the west coast. As I have documented this in other writings, there is no need to go into detail. Suffice it to say that at the time they separate and declare themselves to be independent socialist republics, each will have to smash the existing state apparatus. Otherwise, those who are leading the revolution will merely set themselves up as the new rulers! Out of the frying pan, into the fire!

It may be objected that the newly created, independent republics may not be socialist at all, but a new form of "enlightened" capitalism. To such starry eyed optimists, I can only respond that capitalism is capitalism, capitalists are capitalists, and to use the words "enlightened" and "capitalism" in the same sentence, is an oxymoron, a contradiction in terms. The one and only goal of the capitalists is to make the maximum possible profit, at the expense of the working class. Mind you, there is something to be said for repeating our mistakes, in the sense of setting up a new capitalist independent republic: It is the very height of stupidity!

Of course, the astute reader may well wonder, What Is To Supersede The Smashed State Machine? In fact, Lenin devoted a whole section of his book to that question. He then proceeded to quote Marx, at some length, as he considered it to be of such vital importance:

"The Commune was formed of the municipal councillors, chosen by universal suffrage in the various wards of the town, responsible and revocable at short terms. The majority of its members were naturally working men, or acknowledged representatives of the working class . . . Instead of continuing to be the agent of the Central Government, the police was at once stripped of its political attributes, and turned into the responsible and at all times revocable agent of the Commune. So were the officials of all other branches of the administration. From the members of the Commune downwards, the public service had to be done at *workingmen's wages.* The vested interests and the representative allowances of the high dignitaries of state disappeared along with the high dignitaries themselves.

"Having once got rid of the standing army and the police, the political force elements of the old government, the Commune was anxious to break the spiritual force of repression, the 'parson power' . . .

"The judicial functionaries were to be divested of their (sham) independence . . . Like the rest of the public servants, magistrates and judges were to be elective, responsible and revocable".

No wonder the social chauvinists are so dead set against smashing the existing state machine, and setting up the Dictatorship of the Proletariat! They are determined to set themselves up as the new rulers! The best way to do that is by taking over the existing state apparatus, and using it for their own purposes! That simply cannot be done, under the Dictatorship of the Proletariat! The last thing they want to do is work for the wages of workers! And the very idea of being held accountable and revocable! Such heretical thoughts never occurred to any capitalist!

Under the Dictatorship of the Proletariat, bandits will not be "mollycoddled", to use a popular expression. We cannot force anyone to abide by the law, but we can make everyone wish they had! Those who choose to break our laws will be put to work. As their skills tend to be limited to thievery, perhaps such tasks as building railroads is something they can handle!

In short, the experience of the Paris Commune showed us that the democracy of the capitalists, bourgeois democracy, can and must be transformed into proletarian democracy. This is referred to the Dictatorship of the Proletariat.

This new state apparatus is still necessary, after the revolution, as classes will continue to exist. The resistance of the capitalists will increase ten fold, as they will be in a frenzy of hatred! They will be desperate to restore their "paradise lost"! The idea that the working class might rise up and overthrow them, has never occurred to any billionaire! They are prepared to stoop to any depth, to any subterfuge, in their quest to return to power. Hence the necessity for the Dictatorship of the Proletariat.

One of the reasons for the failure of the Paris Commune is the fact that it did not suppress the resistance of the capitalists, or at least it did not crush them with sufficient enthusiasm. For that matter, the same can be said of the working people of Russia and China, in that after the socialist revolution in each country, they did not sufficiently crush their capitalists. As a result of this, capitalism has been restored in those countries.

This is no reason for despair on our part. It is merely up to us to learn from their mistakes. No doubt the working people of those countries will soon, once again, rise in revolt. They have done it before, they will do it again. Only next time, we can count on them doing a proper job of crushing the capitalists! At that time, the capitalists of both Russia and China will learn the true meaning of the term, Dictatorship of the Proletariat.

Perhaps it is best to go into a little detail. After the death of Stalin, the Russian capitalists were able to return to power. It is to the credit of the Chinese Communists that they took action, in order to prevent a similar restoration of power, by the Chinese capitalists. That action took the form of the Great Proletarian Cultural Revolution.

To further clarify the situation, we can face the fact that "mass motions" take place under socialism, just as they do under capitalism. I refer to this as an Act of God, although most social scientists have a different name for this. To each his own. The point is that the common people of China, which is to say the workers and peasants, were in motion, around the year 1960. The response of the Central Committee of the Communist Party of China was without precedent. The order was given that the police and military were to keep out of this, except in cases of murder, rape or arson.

Perhaps it would be helpful to compare this response, of the Chinese Communist Party, to the response, by the various capitalist governments, to the Occupy Movement, of recent memory. Or perhaps "compare" is not the appropriate word, as there is no comparison. The Occupy Movement spread to a great many countries of the world, all of which are capitalist, and in each case, the response was the same: It was crushed, with varying degrees of brutality.

Yet the fact remains that the Cultural Revolution raged for ten years. During that time, the common people of China were schooled in the class struggle. For that reason, Chairman Mao was of the opinion that any restoration of capitalism, in China, would not last long. As he put it, "at worst, several decades". It has been several decades since the capitalists managed to return to power in China, so the country is overdue for a revolution.

That being said, the fact remains that the ten year Cultural Revolution was just that. Cultural. True, the capitalists were hiding in various fields of culture. It is also a fact that they were also hiding in various fields of science. The Revolution merely touched upon science. Most of the capitalists, who were hiding in science, were not affected. That is at least part of the reason the Chinese capitalists were able to return to power. The Cultural Revolution did not go far enough!

The current generation of young Chinese Communists are going to have to face the fact, no matter how unpleasant, that their parents and grandparents failed to ask the peasants a few key questions. Such as: Describe the dragon! This despite the fact that *the Chinese have named one of the years after the dragon! The Year of the Dragon!* It was a serious oversight.

As is well known, I maintain that the "dragon" is nothing other than the pterosaur, commonly referred to as the pterodactyl. There are numerous other animals which I have identified, including the "lake monster", which is the "walking whale", basilosaurus. Then there is the not so little matter of "water witching". That is a mere selection of numerous details, of which the peasants are well aware, yet rarely mention. It just never occurs to the peasants that the scientists are interested in these things!

Of course, we are entitled to our wildlife, as it is part of our heritage. It should come as no great surprise to anyone that the capitalists are denying us our heritage. It is also a fact that the process known as "water witching", can be modified to generate an abundant supply of electricity. Yet that is secondary to the fact that, during the Cultural

Revolution, the capitalists were able to hide, in various fields of science.

As the capitalists, in those fields of science, were not being challenged and exposed, they were able to get together and plot the best way to return to power. They too have their leaders! So they just bided their time, waiting for the correct moment to strike. Immediately after the death of Chairman Mao, they made their move.

The point is that the people taking part in the Cultural Revolution, managed to overlook the obvious. Perhaps it is because the scientists are held in such high regard, almost universally admired and respected. In popular terms, this is referred to as being placed "on a pedestal". No one should be "placed on a pedestal", if for no other reason than that we are all human, and we all make mistakes.

That in no way changes the fact that the people taking part in the Cultural Revolution, failed to attack a particular group of capitalists, those whom were hiding in science. This may be acceptable for common people, the members of the public, but not for true Marxists, the members of the Chinese Communist Party.

Professional people must be held to a higher standard. That includes the scientists, regardless of the field of expertise. Of course, I am referring to the social sciences. In other words, scientific socialists, true Marxists, Communists, must hold themselves, and each other, to a high standard.

If that statement sounds harsh, it is only because it is harsh. The class struggle calls for harsh measures! The capitalists must not be allowed any peace! To put it in popular terms, if they are "keeping a low profile", "out of sight, out of mind", then it is only because "thieves love darkness"! Thieves do not advertise the burglaries they are planning to commit!

In much the same way, after the revolution, we can expect the capitalists to plot and scheme *in secret*! They are not to be under estimated! They succeeded in restoring capitalism in Russia and China! We must not allow that to happen in America!

To put it in military terms, after the revolution, after they are overthrown, the capitalists will "retreat and regroup". They will then attempt to "counter attack". This must not be allowed. No mercy! Once we have them "on the ropes", "down but not out", then that is the time to "put the boots to them!" (If you will excuse the mixed metaphors.)

At no point have the capitalists ever shown the working people any mercy. We must be every bit as merciless to the capitalists, as they are to us. They must be *crushed, destroyed!* We must not allow them any opportunity to challenge our authority!

This is not to say that we should go to extremes, as the French revolutionaries did, in the Great French Revolution of 1789. Bear in mind that the death penalty is to be used only as an absolute last resort. It is not a matter of being merciful to the capitalists. It is simply a matter of facing the fact that once people are dead, they can no longer be the slightest bit useful.

These facts must be explained to common people, the workers of America. The vast majority are honest, law abiding, tax paying, proud citizens. As such, they tend to think the best of all others. That includes the capitalists. We must be supremely patient with common people, respecting their beliefs. At the same time, we must explain to them that the capitalists are highly skilled liars.

That does not apply to "Marxists", those who are aware of the revolutionary theories of Marx and Lenin, Communists. We must hold such people to a higher standard. Shoddy work must not be tolerated!

No doubt there are some Communists who will take these remarks as a personal insult. It is not meant to be personal, but such a defensive response, on the part of certain people, is to be expected. Yet that is no reason to remain silent, as certain things just have to be said. We must not repeat the mistakes of the Chinese Communists! We must be critical of ourselves and each other!

It is the members of the Communist Party who lead the common people. For that reason we demand more from them. They provide the first line of defence against the capitalists. Membership is voluntary, but comes with a great deal of responsibility. In particular, in the past, it was up to the Communist Party members, of both Russia and China, to prevent the capitalists from returning to power. In this they failed. To repeat: we must learn from their mistakes, so that we can avoid repeating them.

With that in mind, it is necessary for the Party to conduct periodic purges, to get "rid of the driftwood", to cleanse the Party of those who have perhaps lost their enthusiasm. Then there are those who have weaselled their way into the Party, for personal reasons. Both types must be removed from the Party.

The importance of periodic purges must be stressed. For example, immediately before the Russian revolution of November 7, 1917, the Russian Communist Party conducted a purge. At that time, a number of fine Communists were removed from the Party. It was suspected that at the time of the Insurrection, they were likely to lose their nerve. Hence the purge.

It would appear that we have come a long way from the beginning of the article, in which we referred to smashing the existing state apparatus, immediately after the revolution, and so we have. Yet the fact remains that such an action was merely the first step, the beginning of the creation of a new state apparatus:

The Dictatorship of the Proletariat.

CHAPTER 5

Freedom Convoy 2022: Hold the Line!

Feb 25, 2022

The Canadian Truckers Protest, other wise known as the Freedom Convoy 2022, is now entering its third week, as I write this. This began as a protest against a set of rules, in both countries, requiring truckers to be fully vaccinated, before being allowed to cross the border. It has now "snowballed" to include a broader list of grievances, including the removal of the Prime Minister, Justin Trudeau.

The Prime Minister, in turn, is determined to end the blockade. As he stated, it is time to "denounce these illegal acts. They are harming the communities they are taking place in -they are hurting jobs, businesses and our country's economy".

It should be noted that the press is referring to the biggest trucks, the "semi trailers", or "big rigs", as "trucks", while the smaller vehicles are being referred to as "passenger vehicles". So for the purposes of this article, I have chosen to use that terminology.

For the first two weeks, the downtown area of Ottawa, which is the Canadian capital city, was occupied by trucks. The Prime Minister responded by "making himself scarce". Instead of meeting with the protesters, he "moved to an undisclosed location". It would appear that the leader of the Canadian people is afraid of the very people he is leading!

Now the joke among the working people is that we no longer go into a fast food restaurant and order a chicken sandwich. Now we order a "Trudeau sandwich". I rather doubt that our Prime Minister appreciates our sense of humour!

As the occupation of the capital was not getting the attention of our esteemed leader, the protesters decided to adopt sterner measures. One of the main border crossings, between the United States and Canada, that of the Ambassador Bridge, was blocked. This succeeded in getting the attention of the government, on both sides of the border!

There are over one hundred border crossing points, between the United States and Canada. After all, the border stretches 8,891 kilometres or 5,524 miles. Several of these are considered to be major crossing points, or "arteries", from the viewpoint of the business people. The Ambassador Bridge, between the city of Windsor, Ontario, on the Canadian side of the border, to the city of Detroit, Michigan, on the American side of the border, is one of those arteries.

As that is the major auto manufacturing centre, the closure of that Bridge has serious "economic implications". In fact, it is estimated that four hundred million dollars worth of goods flows across the border, each day. With the Ambassador Bridge blockaded, the press reported "some production cuts, shift reduction and temporary plant closures", among the auto manufacturers.

This loss of production is the primary concern of the politicians. They refer to it as "hurting the country's economy". In fact, it cuts into the profits of the capitalists. As the politicians are the devoted servants of the capitalists, that is of course their main concern.

This 'concern" extends to the other side of the border. Even President Biden is worried. The press reports that his "administration" is "monitoring the situation at the border very closely and Cabinet officials were engaged around the clock to bring this to a swift end".

They were not joking. To that end, the Homeland Security Secretary, as well as the Transportation Secretary, have urged their Canadian counterparts to "use federal power to resolve this situation" and offered the support of their departments.

No one is quite sure just what kind of "support" they had in mind. Still less sure are Canadians, concerning the statement by Trudeau, to the effect that officials "have been in close contact with Representatives and officials from the United States to align efforts to resolve this situation". Unless it means that he is nothing more than a lap dog of the Americans!

Perhaps if the Prime Minister would emerge from hiding, out of his "undisclosed location", and meet with the protesters, the very citizens he has been elected to represent, then he would at least earn a little respect. The attitude of the protesters now, with regard to Trudeau, make it abundantly clear that they find him to be contemptible!

Then there is arguably the strangest accusation of all, by certain members of the press, to the effect that the Truckers Protest is "well organized and funded by the alt right".

We beg to differ. The Truckers Protest started out as anything but "well organized"! It appeared in a completely spontaneous manner. It is only now that several leaders have been identified, and they are providing direction to the protest. But then, in any such situation, leaders emerge. The cream always rises to the surface!

Then there is the accusation that it is being "funded by the alt right". No doubt many people are wondering what they are talking about. With that in mind, I conducted a search on the internet. Their "definition" is that it is short hand for "Alternative Right, a loosely connected far right, nationalist movement . . . characterized by rejection of mainstream politics, and by the use of mainline media to disseminate provocative content, often expressing opposition to racial, religious or gender equality."

Now that is more of a condemnation, rather than a definition!

Without a doubt, the Truckers Protest is well funded. As the movement has spread across the country, and even to other countries, it has broad support. People from "all walks of life", which is to say different classes, backgrounds, religions and ethnic groups, have come together to support the protest. The money which is being sent to the protesters, is being put to good use. The trucks are being provided with fuel. As well, food, wood for campfires and propane for cooking, are being provided. Meals are being prepared and given to all, including the homeless. Hotel rooms are being rented, and all are allowed to take showers. First aid is provided, as well as entertainment. The protesters, the people who are benefitting from this wonderful hospitality, are not questioning the source!

Still, Trudeau took the advice of our southern neighbours, and invoked the "Emergencies Act", which is to say that he, effectively, declared martial law. This has never been done before, as it is meant to be used strictly in case of an absolute emergency. It is also *subject to the approval of Parliament!*

In all fairness to our Prime Minister, before invoking the Emergency Act, he said that he spoke to the Premiers of all the provinces. True. Yet he neglected to mention that several of the Premiers were opposed to this!

The American journalists who are covering the protests are mentioning, for the sake of their American viewers, that the Premiers are the "equivalent of the American governors".

In fact, this Emergencies Act has been met with widespread opposition, to put it mildly. The Canadian Civil Liberties Association has vowed to take the Canadian government to court. The Premier of the province of Alberta has promised the same thing. The Premier of the province of Quebec has expressed opposition. This has not stopped Trudeau from ordering the police to clear all protesters from the city of Ottawa, even before the Emergencies Act is approved by Parliament!

It should be noted that the blockade of the Ambassador Bridge, as well as the blockade of other border crossings, was resolved peacefully. All such crossings are now open to traffic. There was no need to resort to Emergency Act measures. The same could almost certainly be done in the city of Ottawa, if the Prime Minister would only meet with the protesters.

Yet Trudeau has his own priorities. The press is reporting he actually stated, that "those who support the Truckers Protest" are "misogynists, racists, women haters, science deniers, the fringe, supporters of swastikas". As all members of the Conservative Party, in Parliament, support the protest, all took that as a personal insult!

In particular, one Conservative Member of Parliament stood up and gave Trudeau an "earful"! She stated that she is a "proud Jewish woman, a descendant of those who have survived the holocaust", and as such, she objected to be called a Nazi! Who can blame her? She then demanded an apology, one which is not forth coming.

It is worth mentioning that the New Democratic Party, NDP, which bills itself as the Party of the "little guy", the working people, even a "socialist" party, is now supporting Trudeau and the Liberal Party, in attempting to crush the Truckers Protest, using the Emergency Act! In so doing, they have managed to show their "true colours"!

Remarkably enough, some of the most accurate reports of the Protests are coming from an American news network which is thought to be very "right wing", which is Fox News. In fact, most of the other established American networks take great delight in "bashing" them, to use a popular expression. Yet the fact is that their reports are accurate, which may well be the very reason they are so passionately hated!

One American journalist, who works for this hated news outlet, and whom has vast experience in reporting on protests, is amazed. He compares it to "two different worlds", in that the protesters are "cooperating with the cops, giving away free food, feeding the homeless". Even more remarkable, the "cops do not want to enforce the law!"

All journalists are agreed that the atmosphere at the protest sites is that of "festival" or "carnival". Families have brought their children. An inflatable playground has been set up in Ottawa. There are even several saunas, despite the fact that the winter temperatures can sink to thirty degrees below zero! There are countless flags on display, most of which are Canadian, but also flags of America and Quebec. People are standing around camp fires, singing the national anthem of both countries, Canada and America. They are also singing and dancing to the music of "We're Not Gonna Take It", and "We Are the World", among others.

When the police show up, they tend to chant "Freedom", lock their arms and chant "Hold the Line!" They refer to the police as their friends! No wonder the American journalists are amazed!

The authorities have responded by setting up a "united command centre", combining police from the RCMP, Royal Canadian Mounted Police, the OPP, Ontario Provincial Police, the Ottawa City Police, and apparently other police forces. They refer to this as combining federal, provincial and municipal police forces.

They are quite concerned with the fact that so many protesters are former members of the police, as well as military veterans. As such, they are well trained, familiar with the tactics of the police, and know precisely how to respond. Worse, those same protesters are encouraging the police to join them!

Without doubt, this stands in stark contrast to protests in America. As yet the Canadian police have not resorted to night sticks, tear gas, pepper spray or water cannons. They certainly have not used "rubber bullets"! There may be a good reason for this. It is entirely possible that should the police be given such an order, they would refuse to obey it! Worse, the police could even join the protesters!

It is also quite possible that the people in charge are well aware of this! That would explain the reason the order has not been given!

It is now three weeks into the protest, and someone has just posted a video on the internet, to the effect that protesters in Ottawa are "not being arrested". He maintains that "protesters are being handcuffed, placed in patty wagons, taken away and within fifteen or twenty minutes, released". He maintains that is the very thing that happened to him! He speaks from experience!

This has yet to be confirmed. If true, then it means that the support of the protesters is much more wide spread, than I at first thought.

A second protester just posted another video on the internet, in which he says he was "roughed up, handcuffed, placed in a paddy wagon, taken away from the protest site and released". Of course he immediately returned to the protest site. As neither individual has any particular reason to lie, it is quite likely that these stories are true.

The implication is that the police may be resorting to "passive resistance". It is entirely possible that, under pressure from their superiors, the police are arresting those whom they have to arrest, or at least "apprehending" them, but instead of charging them, are merely removing them from the protest site, and releasing them.

If this is standard practice, I have never heard of it.

Yet at least four leaders of the protest have been arrested and charged. They may, or may not, be exceptional. They have been charged with "mischief", a charge which one American journalist compared to as something out of "Dennis the Menace". He thought it was quite funny, until he determined that such a charge carries a maximum penalty of ten years in prison. Then he quit laughing.

Yet there can be no doubt that the support for the protesters extends to the police. The Chief of Police, for the city of Ottawa, has just resigned. There are also reports of a Staff Sargent of the Ontario Provincial Police also quitting, apparently in protest. As well, a considerable number of members of various police forces are currently taking vacation time, calling in sick, and taking "stress leave". Many of those whom have worked as police officers for some considerable time, so that they are able to retire and receive a pension, are doing so. A great many others, who have responsibilities, have chosen to remain on duty. To merely quit would place an undue burden upon their families.Yet, it would not take a great deal to "push them over the edge", to get them to join the protest. At that point, the "protest" will be properly called a full scale revolution.

But to return to the comment of the American journalist, to the effect that protests in Canada were of a "different world". There is some truth to this. Consider that which Marx wrote in April 12, 1871, at the time of the Paris Commune, in a letter to Kugelman. Bear in mind that at that time, Marx was living in Britain:

"If you look at the last chapter of my Eighteenth Brumaire, you will find that I say the next attempt of the French Revolution will be no longer, as before, to transfer the bureaucratic military machine from one hand to another, but to *smash* it (italics by Marx) and this is necessary for every real people's revolution on the Continent. And this is what our heroic Party comrades in Paris are attempting".

It is important to bear in mind that Marx distinguished between the countries on the "Continent", which is to say Europe, and countries that were not on the Continent. Of course, he was referring to Great Britain, as a country that was not on the continent.

As Lenin pointed out, at the time Marx wrote this, in 1871, Great Britain was "without militarism and, to a considerable degree, without a bureaucracy". For that reason, a "peoples revolution" was possible "*without* the condition of first destroying the 'ready made state machine'". (italics by Lenin)

We can compare this to the current situation, in which America is equivalent to the countries "on the Continent" in 1871, while Canada is equivalent to Britain at that time.

As that is the case, it is clear that the goal of the next American revolution must be to *smash* the existing "bureaucratic military machine", the state apparatus. On the other hand, as Canada has not embraced militarism, and does not have a great bureaucracy, a "people's revolution" is possible, without "first destroying the ready made state machine". No wonder that American journalist got the impression that he had entered a "different world"! He had indeed entered a different world! A world -Canada- in which there is a distinct possibility of a transition to socialism, without first smashing the existing state apparatus! It may well be a simple matter of "buying out" the bourgeoisie!

In fact it was Marx who stated, quite clearly, that "*under certain conditions*", the workers would "not refuse to buy out" the bourgeoisie. Of course, he did not state precisely those conditions, as he was well aware that the situation could change *radically* and *often,* in the course of revolution. Yet the absence of militarism and bureaucracy were absolutely essential.

The point is that America and Canada present a striking contrast.

On the one hand, America has embraced militarism and bureaucracy, which is to say that they have embraced imperialism. The state apparatus, of that country, must be destroyed. There is no other way a socialist revolution can be successful. Further, that state apparatus can be destroyed only through revolution. The American capitalists, the bourgeoisie, will fight this, to their dying breath. Only then, after the existing state apparatus is destroyed, can a socialist republic be created.

On the other hand, Canada has not embraced militarism and bureaucracy. Now that the "people" are rising up, it is entirely possible to buy out the capitalists, the bourgeoisie, and establish socialism, without first smashing the existing state machine. After all, buying out the capitalists may be so much cheaper than fighting them.

It was President Lincoln who is credited with stating that the best way to destroy our enemies, is by converting them into our friends.

It is one thing to say that something is possible, and even desirable, and something else entirely to say that it is feasible. With that in mind, perhaps it is best to consider that which Lenin had to say on the subject.

As Lenin stated, the necessary conditions for a successful transition to socialism, as in Britain, at the time to which Marx was referring, in 1871, *without smashing the existing state apparatus*, were the following: "1) The absolute preponderance of workers, of proletarians, in the population, owing to the absence of a peasantry 2) The excellent organization of the proletariat in trade unions 3) The comparatively high level of culture of the proletariat, which has been trained by centuries of development of political liberty 4) The old habit of the well organized British capitalists of settling political and economic questions by compromise . . . These were the circumstances which at that time gave rise to the idea that the *peaceful* subjugation of the British capitalists by the workers was possible".

It is safe to say that those four conditions now exist in Canada. The vast majority of the population is now proletarian, as the peasants, or farmers, have been all but wiped out. It is also a fact that the proletariat is quite well organized in trade unions. As for a high level of culture, it has never been higher. Most workers are literate and now have digital devices, or at least have access to them, as well as access to the internet. As the truckers protest has revealed, many of them have gained immediate access to the internet, using those devices. Further, the blockade of the Bridge, as well as the occupation of downtown Ottawa, was resolved through compromise. Very little violence was used. In short, the four conditions required for a successful transition to socialism, in Canada, without first smashing the existing state apparatus, currently exist.

Yet a considerable amount of work needs to be done, in order to prepare the proletariat for socialism, and the subsequent Dictatorship of the Proletariat.

It is clear that the Truckers Protest began quite spontaneously, and resulted in the occupation of several blocks, the "downtown", of the capital city of Ottawa. Yet once the city was properly occupied, the press reports that the protesters were "well organized", with "military style logistics hubs keeping food, fuel and other resources flowing to the encampments, where each block has its own captain and night patrol". They went on to say that "Volunteers open up their homes and hotel rooms for participants to shower and do laundry".

From this I can only conclude that many of the people who are taking part in the protests are well trained. The previous training they received, by the military and police, is being put to good use! Further, the fact that the members of the public are "opening their doors to the protesters, inviting them to shower and do their laundry", proves that the protesters have the broad support of the public.

Although the press has made no mention of this, it is quite possible that the "leaders" were in fact members of a Council, or Soviet, as that is the Russian translation. The revolutionary motion frequently gives rise to such Councils.

The fact that "each block has its own captain and night patrol" supports this possibility. That is precisely the very thing that took place in the Seattle Autonomous Zone.

At the end of three weeks, the police were finally able to clear the protesters, from the streets of Ottawa. On one occasion, tear gas was used, but that could have been an accident on the part of the police. There was talk of rubber bullets being used, but that is quite doubtful. Most protesters chose to pack up and leave the city. Which is not to say that they have given up the struggle. They are merely regrouping. They insist that they are determined to "Hold the Line!"

At one point during the protest, a great many vehicles circled the Ottawa airport. The idea was to disrupt air traffic. This did not have the desired effect, but the point is that the protesters are prepared to adopt different tactics.

Now that Ottawa has been cleared of protesters, the press is reporting -correctly- that the situation is "still fluid, volatile". In fact, the truckers have issued a statement, in the name of the Freedom Convoy 2022, to the effect that even though the leaders have been arrested, "This is a grass roots movement and others will fill their roles. We will continue to Hold the Line. We refuse to bow to abuse of power".

With that in mind, there are already reports of trucker protests in Edmonton, Alberta, in Winnipeg, Manitoba, in Toronto, Ontario, and in Osoyoos, British Columbia. Clearly, the protesters are still determined to "refuse to bow to abuse of power", and indeed they are going to "Hold the Line"!

Everyone is agreed that it started as a protest against a set of unreasonable rules, requiring drivers to be fully vaccinated, before being allowed to cross the international border. Then it "snowballed" to include a broader list of grievances, so that the protesters are now calling for "freedom".

It may well be objected that most of the "truckers" are not so much workers, as "owner operators", which makes them small business owners, middle class, or petty bourgeois. This is true. A valid objection, and this calls for an explanation.

We can start by facing the fact that a great many working class people want to "get ahead", which is the expression they tend to use. Who can blame them? No one wants to live "pay check to pay check"!

The solution of so many working people, or at least the more advanced, is to "go into business". This may involve opening up a small store, perhaps as a commissary, selling novelty items, or providing a service, such as delivery, or buying a machine, such as a taxi, perhaps a logging machine or even a truck, and operating the machine. This is referred to as being an "owner-operator", or a "single phase contractor", and such people become small business owners, technically referred to as petty bourgeois. These are terms with which working people must become familiar.

A more popular expression, and one which is perhaps more accurate, is that of "buying a job"!

All too often, these owner operators, including those whom the press are now referring to as "truckers", are at best, able to earn wages. The expenses of trucks, for example, are considerable. Tires are not cheap. As they put it, money merely "changes hands". After they make the bill payments, they are lucky to "earn wages". These expressions are not mine.

Yet a considerable number of people are able to "get by", at least for a while. But then, it is just a matter of time before a crisis "comes along".

As Lenin put it, "Crises of every kind -economic crises more frequently, but not only these- in their turn increase very considerably the tendency towards concentration and monopoly".

The current crisis has been caused, at least in part, by the Virus, and has in turn, indeed increased "very considerably the tendency towards concentration and monopoly". In other words, the middle class people, the petty bourgeois, including the owner operators, the truckers, are experiencing this "tendency towards concentration and monopoly". In short, they are being forced into bankruptcy. They are going broke.

The reason for this is quite simple. As this crisis is causing a decrease in profits, the capitalists, by whom I mean the billionaires, working through their monopoly corporations, are "squeezing" the "little guy", the small business owners, including the truckers. They are passing the losses onto the truckers.

To put this into perspective -lest we fall into a depression and slash our wrists!- bear in mind that it was Lenin who pointed out that "every great revolution, and a socialist revolution in particular, is inconceivable without . . . a lack of equilibrium and chaos . . . all the elements of disintegration of the old society, which are inevitably more numerous and connected mainly with the petty bourgeois, because it is the *petty bourgeois that every war and crisis ruins first*". (my italics)

In fact, it is not just the truckers who are protesting, although they form the most visible presence. The farmers are also protesting, which explains the presence of a great many tractors, especially on the southern parts of Manitoba and Alberta, close to the American border. These farmers too are middle class, petty bourgeois, and are also going broke.

The "good news"- if you will excuse the poor joke- is that this "Freedom Convoy", or "Truckers Protest", has spread across the country, and even to other countries. As that is the case, it has all the indications of the beginning of a full scale socialist revolution!

As for those who are skeptical, bear in mind that the current situation meets the requirements, set out by Lenin, of a socialist revolution!

The situation is certainly "chaotic". The "elements of disintegration of the old society", which are "numerous and connected mainly with the petty bourgeoisie", are clear for all to see.

The Liberal Party, which bills itself as the "Centrist Party", the "Party of the middle class", as well as the NDP, the "Leftist Party", which is supposed to be the "Party of the little guy", have both turned against the protesters! On the other hand, the Conservative Party, the "Right Wing Party", which is thought to support the capitalists, is supporting the protesters! The roles have been reversed! This is the very definition of "chaos"! Further, it is the petty bourgeois that is being ruined!

This precisely fits the definition of a "great revolution", and a "socialist revolution in particular", as described by Lenin!

This is not to say that this "truckers protest" will naturally lead to a socialist revolution. Such is not the case. The reason for this is quite simple: We live in a class society!

As that is the case, it follows that we are "blessed" with two ideologies, one bourgeois, and the other proletarian. As Lenin pointed out, "in a society torn by class antagonisms, there can never be a non class or above class ideology. Hence, to belittle socialist ideology *in any way,* to *deviate from it in the slightest degree,* means strengthening bourgeois ideology." (italics by Lenin)

Lenin went on to say that the "*spontaneous* development of the labour movement leads to its becoming subordinated to bourgeois ideology" -and the truckers protest is spontaneous- "for the spontaneous labour movement is pure and simple trade unionism . . . and trade unionism means the ideological enslavement of the workers to the bourgeoisie. Hence our task, the task of Social Democracy, is to *combat spontaneity, to divert* the labour movement from its spontaneous, trade unionist striving to go under the wing of the bourgeoisie, and to bring it under the wing of Social Democracy." (italics by Lenin)

I should mention that at the time this was written, Marxists were referred to as "Social Democrats". With that in mind, Lenin added: "Social Democrats lead the struggle of the working class not only for better terms for the sale of their labour power, but also for the abolition of the social system which compels the propertyless to sell themselves to the rich".

No doubt the astute reader will notice that Lenin used the term "our task", the task of conscious people, Marxists, those who are aware of the revolutionary theories of Marx and Lenin. It was not a "slip of the tongue". He meant every word he said!

This is to say that the "Freedom Convoy", also known as the "Truckers Protest", is bound to become "subordinated to bourgeois ideology", unless the people taking part in those protests become class conscious. It started as a protest against unreasonable restrictions against crossing the border, and has since expanded to include the demand that Trudeau step down.

That is a step in the right direction, but only a step. As yet, the protesters are not aware that Trudeau is merely the head of a state apparatus, one set up to protect the capitalists. To replace him with someone else, would merely result in a change of face. The policy of the government, which serves the capitalists, would not change. No doubt the protesters will learn this, from experience.

That awareness can only come with the awareness of the existence of classes, a class of capitalists, bourgeoisie, and a class of workers, proletarians. They also must be made aware that the interests of the two classes are diametrically opposed. That which is in the best interests of one class is in the worst interest of the other class.

In the past, this awareness has come only from intellectuals, most of whom are middle class, petty bourgeois. But then, at that time, it was only the middle class who were able to go to university, to learn about these theories. After all, it was only in university that these theories were taught, and only with a view to distorting them.

Bear in mind that both Marx and Engels were members of the bourgeois intelligentsia. I mention this for the sake of those who are prejudiced against bourgeois intellectuals.

Yet times have changed, and changed dramatically. The invention of the internet has given rise to a revolution in communications! It is a marvel of modern technology! What is more, a great many working people know precisely how to use the internet! They demonstrated their great skill in broadcasting live, from the site of the protests!

It stands to reason that, for the first time in history, it is now possible for the working class, the proletariat, to become class conscious, without the help of middle class intellectuals! Marxist literature can now be downloaded from the internet, onto various digital devices!

May I suggest that workers, by whom I mean all those who are protesting, should read that which is referred to as the "Essential Works of Lenin". These include State and Revolution, Imperialism, the Highest Stage of Capitalism, and What Is To Be Done?

An understanding of those revolutionary works will give protesters a fine grounding in the struggle for scientific socialism, including the Dictatorship of the Proletariat. Bear in mind that, as Lenin stated, "Those who recognize *only* the class struggle are not yet Marxists . . . A Marxist is one who *extends* the acceptance of the class struggle to the acceptance of the *Dictatorship of the Proletariat.*" (italics by Lenin)

We will know that the working class is "getting the message", becoming class conscious, when the expression Dictatorship of the Proletariat becomes common place!

I had hoped that the devastation to the middle class, the petty bourgeois, caused by the Virus, would inspire many of the intellectuals within that class, to embrace those revolutionary theories, and bring that awareness to the working class. That could still happen. In fact, it is just a matter of time. The capitalists will see to that!

In all previous socialist revolutions, the working people did their part. They rose up and demanded change. The trouble was that the working class, the proletariat, were not class conscious, as the conditions of life of the working class, do not lead to the awareness of classes. It was up to conscious people, middle class intellectuals, Marxists, to bring that awareness to the working class. Rest assured, Lenin was one such middle class intellectual!

In much the same way, the working class people taking part in the current protests are not class conscious. This is to be expected.

The fact that conscious people, middle class intellectuals, are not "tripping over themselves" trying to bring this Marxist awareness to the working class, is no cause for "doom and gloom". It is what it is!

It is one thing to accept something. Now it is just a little matter of changing it. And change it we can, and we will! As the middle class intellectuals have as yet failed to perform their duty -and it is their duty to bring to the working class the awareness of the revolutionary theories of Marx and Lenin!- then the working class will just have to educate themselves! There is more than one way to skin a cat!

Now it is a matter of combining theory and practice. A careful reading of the revolutionary theories of Marx and Lenin are one thing, and putting those revolutionary theories to the test, is something else entirely! The Truckers Protest provides us with a golden opportunity!

What does Lenin say about that? "Class political consciousness can be brought to the workers, *only from without* . . . outside of the sphere of relations between workers and employers. The sphere from which alone it is possible to obtain this knowledge is the sphere of relationship between *all* the various classes". (italics by Lenin)

Lo and behold, our cup runneth over! The Truckers Protest involves all the "various classes"! It falls "outside the sphere of relations between workers and employers"! Just what the "doctor ordered"! More accurately, just what "Lenin ordered", as I could not resist that terrible joke!

When Lenin referred to the "sphere of relations between workers and employers", he was referring to the struggle of workers for better wages and working conditions, which goes on constantly. Workers do not have to be told about this, because they constantly experience it!

By contrast, the Truckers Protest is concerned with our democratic rights, including our right to peaceful assembly and protest. It also involves different classes, including the middle class, the petty bourgeois, as most protesting truckers are middle class. Then there were certain middle class people within the city of Ottawa, for example, who were upset, as the protest was hurting their business. After all, it is difficult for a restaurant to compete with those who are giving away free meals!

Of course the ruling class of capitalists, the bourgeoisie, were determined to end the occupation of Ottawa, as they saw it as a threat to the rule of their class.

That pretty well covers the "sphere of relations between all the various classes"!

Now that the Ambassador Bridge is open for business, and the city of Ottawa has been "liberated" from peaceful protesters, the Prime Minister rescinded the Emergency Act. Mind you, the pressure from so many people, including the Premiers of several provinces, as well as the threat of legal action, may have helped to force his hand. For that matter, even though the Emergency Act was approved by Parliament, it also had to be approved by the Senate. The approval of the Senate was not assured.

The events of the last few weeks may prove to be the beginning of a socialist revolution, one which spans two countries. I say this because other such protests are already being planned. A "Peoples Convoy", from California to Washington, DC, is gathering. The National Guard has already been notified. Other protests are in the planning stages.

No doubt the protesters will soon learn to be flexible, and adjust their tactics. There is something to be said for doing the unexpected! Hit the enemy at their weak point! Keep them off balance! Give them no peace!

Above all, study the revolutionary works of Marx and Lenin! Become class conscious! Carry the message to other members of the working class! Join the various mainstream political parties!

Set up stations so that people can become members of the various political parties, and even put their names down as candidates for political office. Those who are computer literate can assist with this.

Run for office! In Canada, run for Parliament! In America, join the two parties, as card carrying members, and run for Congress! Encourage your family and friends to join you! Do not surrender any political office to the capitalists! Extend the protests to the provincial and state capitals! Protest in front of their businesses and homes! Carry the protests to their fancy restaurants and resorts! Leave messages on their luxury vehicles!

There were a great many signs at the Ottawa protest site, but none with class content. With that in mind, may I suggest, as a means of raising the level of awareness of the working class, banners which read:

Workers of the World, Unite!
Dictatorship of the Proletariat!
Scientific Socialism!
Hold the Line!

CHAPTER 6

Canadian Liberals and NDP Attempt Merger

Mar 26, 2022

The current crisis in capitalism is causing the various mainstream political parties to show their "true colours". In fact, both the Liberal Party and the New Democratic Party, NDP, recently opposed the truckers protests, both in the city of Ottawa and at the Ambassador Bridge.

This is significant, as the Liberal Party portrays itself as the Party of the "middle class", while the NDP claims to be the Party of the "little guy", the working class. Further, they would have us believe that working people who can manage to "make ends meet", although with great difficulty, are "middle class". By implication, the working people who are unemployed or under employed, frequently homeless and relying on food banks, are members of the working class. Such is hardly the case!

No doubt many readers are new to the class struggle, as the revolutionary movement has caused countless people to become politically active. As Lenin phrased it, "symptomatic of any genuine revolution is a rapid, tenfold and even hundredfold increase in the size of the working and oppresses masses -hitherto apathetic- who are capable of waging the political struggle, weakens the government, and makes it possible for the revolutionaries to rapidly overthrow it."

As countless working people are now politically active, it is clear that we are facing a "genuine revolution".

It is significant that so many working people refer to this awakening in a slightly different manner. As they phrase it, "We woke up!" The fact that the two mainstream political parties, Liberals and NDP, came together against the very people they claim to represent, shows that they too are in the service of the ruling class of capitalists.

The important thing to bear in mind is that this "awakening", effectively "weakens the government, and makes it possible for the revolutionaries to rapidly overthrow it." In other words, the working class, the proletariat, must overthrow the ruling class of capitalists, seize political power and establish socialism, in the form of the Dictatorship of the Proletariat.

Now that we are blessed with the internet -and the internet is indeed a blessing!- the first impulse of most people, those who are just now becoming politically active, is to use it, to get a definition of the term "working class", as opposed to "middle class".

The response is that of mass confusion. Various definitions are given, mainly with a reference to the amount of money a person earns, over the course of a year. Other definitions include the type of employment, such as that of a labourer or waitress. All are careful to avoid a proper Marxist definition of working class.

With that in mind, it is best to provide a proper Marxist definition of various classes, starting with the working class, the proletariat.

According to Marx, working class people are those who have nothing to sell but their labour power. We work for wages, if for no other reason than the fact that we have no choice in the matter. We are technically referred to as "proletarians", a term with which working people must become familiar. If we are not familiar with this term, the capitalists will use it against us.

Then there are the middle class people, or "petty bourgeois". These are the people who own small businesses, perhaps a corner store or a small shop. They tend to work countless hours, trying to "make ends meet". Others may own a machine, perhaps a taxi or a truck, drive those machines as much as possible, and effectively become "owner-operators". It becomes a constant battle to find work for the machine, and to get paid a decent rate. The trouble being that all such small business owners are in competition with each other, constantly under bidding the other. The end result is that of desperation, generally resulting in bankruptcy.

Another class is that of the peasantry, although in North America they are referred to as farmers. There are even fewer farmers than there are middle class people. Most of the people who previously owned family farms have either been driven into bankruptcy, died or have retired. Very few young people are prepared to take over the burden of a family farm. Most are well aware that there are easier ways to go broke!

Yet many of those few remaining farmers took part in the recent "truckers protest", especially at the border crossings.

That brings us to the monopoly capitalists, the billionaires, technically referred to as the "bourgeoisie". They perform no useful service. They contribute nothing to society. They are mere parasites, leaching off the labour of others. They own all the major banks, mills, mines, factories, railroads, shipping lines, communications networks and anything else of any considerable value. That includes the internet. They are also the class of people who are running the country. Our democratically elected politicians "dance to their tune". The fact that both the Liberals and the NDP opposed the truckers protest, is proof of that!

The capitalists do not want the working class, the proletariat, to become aware of themselves as a class. After all, the class interests of the working class and that of the capitalists are diametrically opposed. That which is in the best interests of the working class is in the worst interests of the capitalist class. It is in the best interests of the capitalists to pay the working class as little as possible, while working us as hard as possible. Of course, precisely the opposite is in the best interests of the working class.

But as the capitalists own the internet, they are careful to spread as much confusion as possible. It is to be hoped that the proper Marxist definition of classes will prove to be helpful.

But now to return to the subject of the political parties in Canada. Aside from the Liberal and NDP, there are three other mainstream political parties. These are the Conservative Party, the Green Party, and the Bloc Quebecois. The Conservatives refer to themselves as the "Party of Business", while the Bloc Quebecois is active only in Quebec.

The Green Party is apparently an alternative to the other mainstream political parties. It is somewhat strange, to put it politely. It has four "organizational pillars", which include "ecological wisdom, social justice, grass roots democracy, and non violence". Perhaps someone should let the Greens know that most Canadians have no idea about the first three, but as for the fourth, that of non violence, may I suggest a reality check? Canada is a country which was built on violence! Most Canadians have firearms, and are fully prepared to use them!

That in no way changes the fact that the Green Party is one of the mainstream Parties, and it has a following.

As that is the case, and as it is further my opinion that all Canadians should become politically active, then I maintain that it is one of the Parties that all Canadians should join. In fact, I think that all Canadians should join all the mainstream political Parties, or at least as many as possible.

The reason I say this is because it is the members of the Party who set the Party policy, elect leaders of the Party, and determine the candidates for any and all political office. Becoming a member of any Party is simplicity itself, according to the internet. As it is stated:

> "Requirements to join a political party:
>
> "You must agree with the general principles of the party (they will often get you to sign or tick a box online stating that you agree)
>
> "Most parties will not allow you to join if you are a member in another party (there is no way for them to police this, they rely on the honour system)
>
> "You must be a resident of Canada (no, you don't even need to be a citizen, just a resident of Canada)
>
> "You must be a minimum age (this differs between political parties, but is usually as low as 14 or 16; so if you are in high school, you can be a member of a political party with all the rights that come with it- which includes voting in a nomination race)

"Joining is easy! The membership of a political party is the bread and butter of the party. So the parties make it super easy for you to join online. The membership fees for the political parties differ."

It goes on to say that the membership fees for the Conservative Party are the highest, at $15. per year. The Green Party comes in at $10. per year, the Bloc Quebecois at $5. per year, while the Liberal Party is free. The membership in the NDP varies, depending upon the province in which you live.

Those membership rates are well within the means of most Canadians. If nothing else, people can at least join the Liberal Party, as it is free. Better yet, people of high school age can join, as it is best to encourage people to become politically active, as soon as possible.

My suggestion is that as many Canadians as possible, join as many political Parties as possible, and become as politically active as possible. When applying for membership in more than one Party, feel free to be naughty. Just "tick the little box" that says you are not a member of any other political Party. There is a certain sense of urgency in this.

The fact is that the NDP is in the process of forming an alliance with the Liberals. The leader of the NDP, Jagmeet Singh, has met with the leader of the Liberals, Justin Trudeau, our current Prime Minister, and that is their plan. Further, they want to increase the military spending, presumably to get more involved with NATO. This increase in military spending will almost certainly coincide with an increase in bureaucracy, so that Canada will end up embracing imperialism. They must be stopped!

The two leaders, by themselves, cannot officially come to any "formalized agreement". It must be endorsed by the members of both parties, the "rank and file". That is the reason it is so important, even urgent, that many Canadians join those two Parties.

As mentioned in a previous article, Lenin pointed out that in a country which does not embrace militarism and bureaucracy, it is possible to have a revolution, without destroying the "ready made state apparatus". It is simpler and cheaper to "buy out" the capitalists. Yet once the country embraces militarism and bureaucracy, then the state apparatus must be destroyed. This makes the revolution far more difficult.

As for those who dispute that previous statement, may I suggest taking a close look at the revolutionary movement in America. All protests are met with the utmost brutality. That includes tear gas, pepper spray, clubs, water cannons and even "rubber bullets".

An American journalist, one who has extensive experience in covering protests in America, compared the recent truckers protests in Ottawa, as being "in a different world". The protesters were treated with respect. The occupation of the city, as well as of Ambassador Bridge, was dealt with in a manner which involved a minimum of violence.

Yet if Trudeau and Singh have it their way, that will all change. Protesters will then be treated the same way they are treated in America. Then the revolution will be far more difficult, far more bloody, as the existing state apparatus will then have to be destroyed.

The best way to stop them is by having as many Canadians as possible, joining the two Parties, Liberal and NDP. Of course, feel free to join the other Parties also. Encourage your friends and families to join. Those who are familiar with computers can assist those who are not. As members of the Parties, you can take part in setting policy. Choose someone from among yourselves to run for any and all political offices. Go on Facebook, and all other social media outlets, and encourage people to also join the Parties. No doubt all schools, including high schools, will be interested. The more people who join the Parties, the better.

Bear in mind, that the main thing is to raise the level of awareness of the working class, to get people politically active. The more people we send to Ottawa, the better. We want to stop the country from embracing militarism and bureaucracy. In the process of becoming politically active, working class people will learn that the capitalists are in charge, and have to be overthrown. Whether this will involve violence or not, largely depends upon the capitalists.

Those who become politically active now, possibly by taking part in protests or by joining the various political Parties, preferably both, will gain valuable experience in the class struggle. It is to be hoped that a great many people who are currently protesting, will join the Parties and choose one of their own to run for Parliament. Assuming enough people do this, all across Canada, then Ottawa will soon be flooded with Leftist people. Of course the same is true for the provincial and territorial capitals.

After the revolution, the capitalists will be overthrown and working class people will be placed in positions of authority, under the Dictatorship of the Proletariat. Any training they receive now will prove to be most valuable.

CHAPTER 7

Concerning "Sacred" Scientific Theories

The current state of science has degenerated to the point that there are certain scientific theories which are not to be challenged. Any students of science whom even suggest that any of these theories is faulty, is promptly punished, by failing any course they may be taking. As well, anyone with a degree in science who spouts such "heresy", is not allowed to earn a living, working in any field of science.

Yet aside from these basic "sacred theories", scientists are allowed to speculate, to dream up other theories, to their "hearts content". This has given rise to various "hare brained" notions, which are put forward, in the name of science. As a result of this, different science books say different things, and science has been reduced to an absurdity. Yet all books of science are agreed that there are certain scientific theories which are correct.

In all fairness to the various books of science, all have one thing in common. In this, they are all mistaken.

Perhaps the most cherished of all the "sacred" scientific theories, is that of the "mass extinction of dinosaurs". This bit of nonsense was first put forward by Luis Alvarez, a famous scientist, a physicist, who suggested that a huge meteor had hit the planet, perhaps sixty five million years ago. He further suggested that, as a result of this impact, all of the dinosaurs had simply dropped dead.

Alvarez was a fine scientist, highly respected. The work that he did in his chosen field, that of physics, was excellent. For that reason, people listened closely to that which he said. That was somewhat unfortunate, as he was also human. In fact, all too often professional people make the mistake of expressing their opinion, concerning a subject of which they know nothing. Alvarez knew nothing about dinosaurs. That meteor, of sixty five million years ago, certainly did *not* wipe out the dinosaurs.

Alvarez was very likely correct, when he suggested that a huge meteor struck the planet, many millions of years ago. Such meteors are rocks from outer space. They are constantly striking the planet. Most of them are the size of a grain of sand, and immediately burn up in the atmosphere. They are commonly referred to as "shooting stars". Others are bigger, and hit the earth, occasionally doing some damage. Then there is the odd huge rock, which may cause wide spread devastation. That is a far cry from causing the mass extinction of countless species of animals!

Yet this theory was embraced by countless members of the public. Who can blame them? It has a certain romantic appeal. The idea is that all huge, terrifying, prehistoric animals, were killed by a rock from outer space! In this manner, the world was made safe for people! If nothing else, the theory sold a great many magazines!

The implication, that the mass extinction of dinosaurs was an Act of God, is quite agreeable to most common people. It is quite preferable to the belief in the theory of evolution!

That in no way changes the fact that the theory of the mass extinction of dinosaurs, is merely a fairy tale. Yet what are dinosaurs?

For many years, scientists have been aware that dinosaurs laid eggs. The discovery of the fossilized remains of countless dinosaurs eggs leaves no room for any doubt! Yet the laying of eggs is characteristic of reptiles, as well as birds. But it is only birds that have feathers. The trouble being, that feathers do not fossilize. So how to prove that dinosaurs had feathers, and were therefore birds?

Fortunately, it is not just the fossilized eggs and bones of dinosaurs which have been discovered. The fossilized remains of the hides of various species of dinosaur have also been found. This is significant, because the "feather follicles" -to use the scientific term- from which all new feathers grow, have also fossilized.

With feather follicles in mind, recently the scientists had the brilliant idea of examining the fossilized remains of hides, of various dinosaurs, under a microscope. To their astonishment, they determined that these fossilized hides did indeed have fossilized feather follicles. Further, from the size, shape and distribution of these feather follicles, they are able to determine the size, shape and even the colour of the feathers, on these dinosaurs. Not only does this prove that dinosaurs were birds, but we also know the colour of their feathers! As birds certainly still exist, and birds are dinosaurs, then dinosaurs cannot be extinct! This proves that the theory of the mass extinction of dinosaurs is a myth! A fairy tale!

This in no way changes the fact that, as Robert Bakker stated in his book, Dinosaur Heresies, "dinosaurs are incontrovertibly dead". This despite the fact that he also states that "birds are dinosaurs"! Dinosaurs cannot be both dead and alive! Yet Bakkar is recognized as an authority in his field. His book is considered to be the "bible" of paleontology!

For that reason, modern day scientists have been forced to resort to verbal gymnastics, in an effort to reconcile the irreconcilable, to explain that even though dinosaurs are extinct, birds are dinosaurs! The alternative is career suicide!

Along with the theory of the mass extinction of dinosaurs, is the theory of the mass extinction of flying reptiles, technically referred to as pterosaurs, commonly referred to as pterodactyls. I use the expression "along with", because some scientists have classified these flying reptiles as dinosaurs, while others do not. Yet all are agreed that they went extinct at the same time that the dinosaurs went extinct.

These flying reptiles are certainly not extinct! Here too, we have a situation in which all scientists are agreed that there has never been any mass extinction of reptiles, even though there was a mass extinction of flying reptiles! *They cannot have it both ways!* Feel free to face the fact that flying reptiles are not extinct!

Further, they are located on six continents of the world, which means that they are not on the Antarctic. It remains to be seen, if they have managed to spread to various islands.

In most parts of the world these animals, flying reptiles, are called "Dragons", although in North America the most common local name is that of "Thunder Bird". The pterodactyls are no more extinct than dinosaurs -birds- are extinct!

Another "sacred" theory is that of the mass extinction of huge swimming reptiles, including mosasaurs, plesiosaurs and ichthyosaurs. This despite the fact that ichthyosaurs were warm blooded animals, which gave birth to live young! So how can they be reptiles? Another awkward question! One that the scientists are not at all anxious to face!

Strangely enough, no scientist has even attempted to explain the reason for the "mass extinction" of these huge swimming reptiles. This stands in stark contrast to the theories provided for the "mass extinction of dinosaurs". If nothing else, we are spared the recital of another fairy tale!

This brings us to that most glaring of absurdities, that of the "mass extinction of mega fauna", here in North America, at the end of the third, and last, ice age.

The scientists would have us believe that the "mega fauna", (huge animals), by which they mean the woolly mammoth, sabre toothed cat, Jefferson ground sloth, dire wolf and short faced bear, all dropped dead, because they could not handle climate change! This despite the fact that those species survived three ice ages! So what happened the first time the climate changed? More awkward questions for the scientists!

Other inconvenient facts also come to mind. One such fact is that the Jefferson ground sloth is named after the third American president, Thomas Jefferson. Even though it went extinct at the end of the last ice age, it was alive at the time of Jefferson! Imagine that!

That brings us to the dire wolf, which even the scientists admit is still alive, even though it is extinct. They refer to this as "a remnant population of an extinct species"!

There was a time, not too long ago, when a species was either extinct, or not extinct. In those days, as long as one member of a species was still alive, then the species was not extinct. Yet that all changed recently, with the advent of the age of "alternative facts"!

The next item on our hit parade is that of "climate change", in the form of "global warming". All scientists are agreed that the industrial revolution gave rise to the whole sale burning of "fossil fuels", and that this, in turn, is causing the world to become considerably warmer.

This neat little theory conveniently overlooks a few little details. The fact of the matter is that the climate is constantly changing! This has been going on since the creation of the planet, and if nothing else, is responsible for the fact that we have four seasons! We have no reason to expect the climate to remain constant! That is not about to happen!

This is not to say that the climate changes equally, on all the continents, at the same time. It does not. Different continents experience different rates of climate change.

As mentioned earlier, the continent of North American recently experienced no less than three ice ages. On three occasions, the continent cooled off, to the point that glaciers covered the continent. Also on three occasions, the continent warmed up, so that those glaciers melted. Continental climate change! It just so happens that we are fortunate to be living at a time in which North America is warm.

Another scientific theory, to which all scientists are agreed, is that there was a time when whales walked on land. True. But then, they would have us believe that around fifty million years ago, all whales took to the water, and lost their legs, over a period of many millions of years. Not exactly. One species of whale still has legs, still walks on land, still grazes, still eats vegetation. It is a predator, but not a carnivore, an omnivore. It eats flesh as well as vegetation. That whale is basilosaurus.

This particular whale has given rise to various myths and legends. Perhaps the most famous of these legends is that of the Loch Ness Monster of Britain. Then too, here in North America, we have the legend of Ogopogo, the monster in Okanagan Lake. A great many people have seen these animals. Yet the scientific community is unanimous in dismissing all of these sightings, as the product of "overly active imaginations".

This in no way changes the fact that there are a number of people, at least in Britain, who are taking these sightings seriously. They are determined to prove the existence of this animal, very likely at their own expense. For this they deserve a great deal of credit!

The reports are that they are using boats and submersibles, complete with underwater cameras, during the day time. Also radar and sonar. As yet, they have come up "empty handed", and with good reason. These whales are nocturnal!

This is to say that basilosaurus spends the day light hours inside caves. Also the winter months. Yet they are predators, and as such have a keen sense of smell. Just as all predators are far more likely to attack when they smell blood, so too these whales come out of the caves, during the day time, whenever they smell blood. That helps to explain the occasional daytime sightings of these animals.

Yet as previously mentioned, these animals are omnivores. They eat vegetation, as well as flesh. This makes complete sense, as the fact is that a fresh water lake cannot possibly support a population of huge whales. There is simply not enough nourishment in the water! It is not the lake, by itself, which supports these whales, but the ecosystem!

The ecosystem consists of the lake, along with the caves, the streams which flow into the lake, and the adjacent woodlands, swamps and meadows. During the warm months, the whale comes out of the water, after sun down, and grazes. It consumes vegetation, mainly grass, no doubt.

The only reason no one has located this whale, is because no one is looking at the meadows. It is very likely that a simple trail camera could detect them, in the moon light.

It is also note worth that the health of the ecosystem depends largely upon the top predator. The experience of Yellowstone National Park proves that!

In that case, the park managers decided to kill all the wolves in the park. As a result of this, the grazing animals, and in particular the elk, very nearly turned the park into a desert. In desperation, the park managers were forced to import some wolves, at great expense, in order to restore the balance of nature.

Happily, this worked, so that the wolves, as top predator, tore into the herds of grazing animals. The balance of nature, within the park, was restored. Yellowstone was saved.

The point is that we must first prove the existence of basilosaurus, the top predator in these huge lakes, and then protect them. The health of the whole ecosystem depends on this!

This brings us to several separate species of humans, which all the scientists agree are extinct. They are not.

The idea that our species, that of homo sapiens, is unique, has a certain appeal, especially to common people. It must also have a certain appeal to the scientists, as it is deeply entrenched in the scientific literature. They would have us believe that even though various species of humans evolved, we are the one and only species of human to survive. Not true!

The fact of the matter is that a species of ape, known as Gigantopithecus, managed to achieve bipedal locomotion, which is to say that they started to walk on two legs, and then, with their forelimbs free for labour, evolved the opposable thumb. They can touch their finger tips with their thumbs! Bipedal apes, complete with the opposable thumb, are the very definition of human! At least, that is my definition of human.

These people, whom I refer to as Giants, live among us, here in North America. They are seen on a regular basis, and are commonly referred to as "Bigfoot" or 'Sasquatch". I refer to them as Giants, a name which is meant to be more accurate, without being derogatory.

This prejudice against all other species of human, helps to explain the attitude of the scientists, concerning a recently discovered species of human, in South Africa, which lived possibly 200,000 years ago. The scientists have given that species the name of Homo Naledi.

Arguments have been made that the brain size of Homo Naledi, that of 600 cc, in that cc stands for cubic centimetres, is too small to be that of a human.

The brain size of our species, Homo Sapiens, is around 1400 cc. The scientists point out that the brains of our closest living relatives, that of chimpanzees, is a mere 400cc, so that a brain of 600cc is too small to be human. Such is hardly the case!

Yet it is broadly accepted, at least among the scientific community, that there was a species of human which lived on the island of Flores, many years ago, referred to as Homo Floresiensis. Their brain size was about 400cc, around that of the size of brains of chimps, yet they were unquestionably human.

It is also a fact that the brain size of Pygmies- although they tend to refer to themselves as Bambuti or Mbuti- is around 400cc, also the same size as that of chimpanzees. Yet without doubt, Pygmies are human. No one disputes that fact! The point being that "human" is not determined by the size of the brain. Now if only the scientists could face that fact!

Incidentally, the brain size of another species of human, that of Neanderthals, is estimated to be even larger than our own, coming in at 1500cc. Yet that is another species of human, which the scientists insist is extinct. Not likely!

This brings us to the most passionately defended bit of scientific hog wash, which is the claim, put forward by various scientists, as well as all government officials, that men *walked on the moon! Nonsense!*

It is Adolf Hitler who is credited with making the statement that "If a lie is big enough, then people will believe it." The lie that "men walked on the moon", certainly qualifies as one of the all time great lies! A true whopper!

But now let us consider the facts which make it impossible to travel to the moon.

First of all, the earth is a giant magnet, and as such, creates a huge magnetic field, which circles the planet. This is a good thing, to put it mildly. Without that magnetic field, we would all be dead!

In scientific jargon, this magnetic field gives rise to something referred to as the Van Allen Belt, which wraps around the earth, much as a protective blanket. This Belt, or blanket, blocks most of the radiation from the sun, which allows life to exist on our planet. Without that Belt, we would be bombarded with massive doses of radiation.

Yet the scientists would have us believe that astronauts passed through this Van Allen Belt, on their trip to the moon. If that was the case, they would have been exposed to massive doses of radiation, which would have quickly killed them. Perhaps not immediately, but within a few days.

No doubt, many skeptical readers will check on the internet- as I did- in the interest of conducting a proper investigation. With that in mind, may I suggest clicking on the article titled: "Yes, Apollo Flew Through the Van Allen Belts Going to the Moon."

I recommend this article because it provides a very clear cut explanation of the reason that it is *not* possible to fly men to the moon. Feel free to disregard the title, as the facts presented within the article proves precisely the opposite.

In this video, which runs for a length of eleven minutes, seven seconds, a lovely young lady, a fine actor, explains that "the earth, which is nothing other than a huge magnet, creates a magnetic field. This magnetic field, which is referred to as the Van Allen Belt, acts as a protective envelope", one which "traps most of the radiation from the sun". An instructive drawing is thoughtfully provided, as a means of illustration. It is further explained that without this "protective envelope", the "earth would be bombarded with massive doses of radiation, which would kill all life on earth". Or at least it would kill us!

Excellent! So far so good!

She went on to say that the "scientists of the time", fifty years ago, "were well aware that the only way the astronauts could get to the moon, was by passing through this Van Allen Belt, and in the process, soaking up massive doses of radiation". Of course, after they passed through the Van Allen Belt, "they would then be exposed to even more radiation, all of which was sure to kill them". This too is true!

Once again: Excellent!

That explanation, which is stated in very clear, simple terms, should provide non technical people -and most working people are non technical- with a basic understanding of the importance of the magnetic field of the planet. It also explains that it is impossible to fly to the moon, without getting killed!

Bear in mind that this young lady is not a physicist, but an actor. No doubt she was paid to read a script, probably with the help of a teleprompter, and she did a fine job! If I was working in the field of entertainment, I would not hesitate to hire her! She knows how to deliver a speech! She certainly earned her pay!

The point being that we cannot hold her responsible for the nonsense which followed! She was merely reading from a teleprompter!

It is very likely that the scientists were forced to hire this young lady, as they could not find any scientist who was prepared to stoop to the hypocrisy of reciting the nonsense which followed! At least, not with a straight face!

It was the scientific writers who deliberately led with a few basic facts, followed by a vast amount of detailed technical information, in an attempt to confuse people. Buried within that mountain of gobbledegook, was a jewel of a detail, which is referred to as "shielding of the space craft".

I can only stress that she was reading from a teleprompter. She went on to explain that, "in order to protect the astronauts from the radiation which was sure to kill them", there was a "Radiation shielding to the space craft, especially to the main command module, where the crew would be spending most of their time".

Nonsense!

The scientists would have us believe that the astronauts went to the moon, through the Van Allen Belt, and were protected from the radiation of the sun, by a "protective shield". *Such a protective shield does not exist!* There is no such substance! It does not exist now, and did not exist fifty years ago! There is no way that astronauts could possibly have gone to the moon, without being exposed to massive doses of radiation! That radiation would have killed them!

Yet to this day, the scientists, and all government officials, insist that "men walked on the moon"! This despite the fact that it cannot be done, without a "protective shield", which does not exist! Duh!

It is quite possible that this lie may go down in history as the ultimate absurdity!

The "theories" which I have listed are the "theories" that common people can help to disprove, quite simply and easily. Feel free to become active and do the work of the scientists! It may help to think of this as part of the revolutionary motion, if only because that is precisely the case!

In other writings, I have detailed the simple steps which must be taken, in order to disprove these fairy tales. I see no reason to repeat them.

There are other scientific theories -fairy tales- which the scientists have chosen to embrace, or face career suicide. These include the "existence of dark matter and dark energy". That implies the existence of a fifth fundamental force in the universe!

More nonsense!

Sadly, the state of science has regressed to a point which can be compared only to that which existed before Newton and Darwin. This is to say that modern scientific enquiry no longer exists.

The problem is one of capitalism, at least capitalism in its final, most rotten stage of monopoly, technically referred to as imperialism. As Lenin stated, imperialism is "reaction, right down the line". The imperialists, in the form of the monopoly capitalists, the billionaires, the bourgeoisie, can and must be overthrown. Until they are overthrown, there will be no progress in any field of science.

It is the working class, the proletariat, which is destined to overthrow that most reactionary class, and crush them, under the Dictatorship of the Proletariat.

The revolutionary motion is growing ever stronger, at least here in North America. It is just a matter of time, and probably a short time, before it breaks out into open rebellion.

With that in mind, I can only offer a word of friendly advice to the scientists and government officials, those who persist in propagating those ridiculous theories. Feel free to "come clean", to admit that it is all a pack of lies. After all, any day now, the truth will be revealed. Better to "cut your losses", to join the working class in overthrowing the bourgeoisie. Help to establish the Dictatorship of the Proletariat!

Your education and experience can be put to good use. Feel free to share with the working people, the revolutionary theories of Marx and Lenin. Let them know what you have gone through, in your years of service to the capitalists. Tell people how you degraded yourself, spreading lies, in the interests of maintaining your career. Your past will not be held against you.

Bear in mind that the alternative is to oppose the revolution, to continue to defend the bourgeoisie. In that case, you can expect to become a target of the revolution. The working class cannot force you, or anyone else, to do the right thing. Yet we can make you wish you had!

Choose wisely. Otherwise, do not be surprised if, after the revolution, you end up in the same remote work camp as that of your former lords and masters, the bourgeoisie. You may then find yourself performing the same manual labour, which could well involve pick and shovel. You have been warned.

CHAPTER 8

Professor Power

Dec 20, 2021

As is well known, the Communist Manifesto was written in 1848. At that time, Marx and Engels were well aware that after the successful socialist revolution, it would be necessary to have "the proletariat organized as the ruling class". Of course, they had no idea of the precise form this organization would take, as they had no experience of any such successful revolution. That changed dramatically with the appearance of the Paris Commune, in the spring of 1871.

Although the Commune was brief, lasting a mere few weeks before it was crushed, with great brutality, Marx subjected it to a most careful analysis in The Civil War In France. Perhaps the most important lesson he drew from this French Revolution, was the fact that the workers cannot merely lay hold of the existing state machine and use it for their own purposes. Instead, it has to be smashed, and replaced with a new state apparatus, in the form of the Dictatorship of the Proletariat. This fact is well known to the social chauvinists, the revisionists. Which is *not* to say that they have embraced this revolutionary Marxist theory. On the contrary, they avoid any mention of this, unless of course it involves distorting the theory. After all, they have their own agenda, which includes taking over the state apparatus, at the time of the revolution, and setting themselves up as the new rulers. The destruction of the existing state machine is the last thing the social chauvinists want to see!

I mention this because it is of such vital importance. Yet Marx went on to say more: "Having once got rid of the standing army and the police, the physical force elements of the old government, the Commune was anxious to break the *spititual force of repression*, the 'parson power'". (my italics)

The point is that the bourgeois state apparatus consists of more than just the "physical force elements", that of police, standing army -National Guard-, prisons and various "correctional institutions". It also consists of numerous "spiritual forces of repression", and that too has to be smashed, *as it is part of the state apparatus!* Marx referred to this as "parson power". It may help to think of these "spiritual forces of repression" as "invisible chains", and these chains have to be broken.

These "spiritual forces of repression" assume many forms. In China, at the time of the revolution, the peasants were rising up and overthrowing the landlords. As they had been crushed and exploited by the landlords for centuries, they lived in mortal dread of those people. With good reason, I might add. For that reason, it was not enough to separate the landlords from their wealth and property. The peasants also placed "dunce hats" on the landlords and paraded them through the streets, mocking and humiliating them. It was in this way that the "spiritual force of repression", the invisible chains of the landlords, was smashed.

If we compare that to the American Revolutionary War of 1776, then it is safe to say that the Chinese landlords "got off easy". In the American revolution, the British Nationalists, the "Tories", those who were crushing and exploiting the American Colonials, were first coated with tar and feathers, before being paraded though the streets. Lo and behold, the invisible chains of the Tories were broken!

Of course, such behaviour is considered to be socially unacceptable, under non revolutionary situations. Yet in times of revolution, the polite customs of civilized society tend to "fall by the wayside".

The fact remains that all "spiritual forces of repression", all invisible chains, have to be smashed. In China, it was the landlords who held such a sway over the peasants. In the American colonies, it was the Tories who terrorized the colonials. Both were dealt with, rather harshly, by the common people, the members of the public. In both cases, the result was the same. The invisible chains were broken.

The current situation in North America is similar, in that there are numerous Mobsters, or members of "Organized Crime", to use the politically correct expression, who make a career of terrorizing and exploiting the working people. One of their favourite methods consists in extorting "protection money" from small business owners, a form of "insurance", to keep their lives and property safe. Those who do not "pay up", generally live to regret this, but not all. Some do not live to regret it!

No doubt, at the time of the approaching American revolution, the "spiritual force" exerted by these mobsters will also be broken. It is very likely that they will experience something worse than tar and feather!

A more subtle form of spiritual repression is exercised by the intellectuals who are responsible for the school text books. Many of them, if not all, are professors at various Universities. For that reason, I refer to them as University Professors, and they possess considerable spiritual power, which I refer to as "Professor Power".

The source of this spiritual power comes not from the terror inspired by the threat of brute force, as per the Mobsters, still less from the threat of everlasting damnation, as per the Clergy, but from the absolute respect, which is demanded by these intellectuals. The University Professors have established themselves as a force which is above reproach. They have set themselves up "on a pedestal", and the scientific theories which they have endorsed are not to be challenged. They have managed to gather to themselves a considerable amount of power, through their control of the educational system. Perhaps a few examples will serve to illustrate this.

All scientists are agreed that there was a mass extinction of dinosaurs, sixty five million years ago. As far as the theory of the mass extinction of dinosaurs is concerned, that is about the only point upon which they are agreed! Some science books insist that dinosaurs were land dwelling reptiles. Others insist that this included flying reptiles. Still other books of science insist that swimming reptiles were also dinosaurs. The scientists are also deeply divided over the cause of this extinction. The most widely held belief is that of a "killer rock from outer space". That has captured the imagination of countless common people! That is more popular than the theory of continental drift, "galloping continents", which carried diseases in their wake! Let us not forget the theory that the dinosaurs grew too big, so that they were unable to have sex, thus could not reproduce! That one has got to be my favourite! To think that such nonsense is put forward in the name of science! It is nothing short of an embarrassment! But then perhaps the scientist who dreamed up this "theory" is on drugs, some real good stuff. We should all be so lucky! No need to be greedy! Feel free to share!

Of course the only reason that the scientists cannot give a rational explanation for the mass extinction of dinosaurs, is because there is none! There was no mass extinction of dinosaurs! Most of the animals which have been classified as dinosaurs, were birds! Others were reptiles! Yet there was evolution, so that over the course of many millions of years, many species of birds evolved, so that new species came into existence.

Then too, there were the reptiles, some of whom have also been classified as dinosaurs. They too have evolved, but as they are cold blooded animals, they evolve much more slowly than birds. They remain largely unchanged.

All scientists are also agreed that we are the one and only species of human still walking the earth. All eye witness reports of another species of human, that of Gigantopithecus, commonly referred to as Sasquatch, Bigfoot or Giants, are calmly and quietly disregarded.

Then there is the theory of the "mass extinction of mega fauna", in which huge animals, including the woolly mammoth and sabre toothed cat, dropped dead, at the end of the last ice age, because they "could not survive climate change". The fact that these animals survived three ice ages, which included several changes in climate, is also ignored!

Of all the denials, by the scientists, perhaps the most common place, is that of the existence of "UFO's", or "Unidentified Flying Objects". Regardless of the number of reliable eye witness accounts, the scientists still maintain that they do not exist! In terms of being stubborn, they put mules to shame!

In fact, this "glow in the night sky" is nothing other than the bioluminescent lights emitted from the hides of the male pterosaurs, also known as pterodactyls, as they display during mating season. Yet as the scientists still maintain that those flying reptiles went extinct, many millions of years ago, they disregard all such sightings! Their capacity for self delusion is an absolute marvel!

This brings me to another theory upon which all scientists are agreed, and that is the fact that there was a time, fifty million years ago, when whales walked on land. True! But then they are still walking on land! Walking whales! Twenty meters long, or sixty five feet, so that they are quite hard to miss. Yet the scientists have managed! I have to give them credit!

These "walking whales" are the source of various "myths and legends", of which the Loch Ness monster is the most famous. Also the "Ogopogo" of Okanagan Lake fame, although the animal is located in a great many large fresh water lakes, in Europe as well as in America. They come out of the water after sun down to graze, to eat grass, so that locating them should not be terribly difficult.

That is a mere selection of the various lies which are contained in the school text books. Students of all ages, from grammar school to university level, are required to memorize this nonsense, these "fairy tales", as a means of earning a diploma or degree. That is sad. It is also "spiritual power". This power, which I refer to as Professor Power, is not to be underestimated!

The common people have been told, all their lives, that the key to success is through education. There is some truth to this, as in a highly industrialized country, illiteracy is a severe handicap. Yet at the same time, the school text books have been written by the University Professors. The one and only way a person can pass all the courses and earn a degree, and in turn become successful, is by first memorizing all the information which is contained in those text books.

This information is certainly not limited to science. The history books are also filled with distortions and out right lies. The point being that the "key to success" lies in not "rocking the boat", not pointing out the lies and hypocrisy contained within these text books, all of which have been written by the University Professors. That is real power!

As for those who suspect that perhaps I am overstating the matter, may I refer you to a speech given by Lenin in August of 1918, less than one year after the successful Russian socialist revolution: "The working people are thirsting for knowledge because they need it to win. Nine out of ten of the working people have realized that knowledge is a weapon in their struggle for emancipation, that their failures are due to lack of education . . . they see how indispensable education is for the victorious conclusion of their struggle."

Under the current political situation, that of capitalism, Lenin pointed out that the schools are nothing but "an instrument of the class rule of the bourgeoisie". Their purpose is to provide the capitalists with "obedient lackeys" and "able workers". Those who properly commit to memory all the distortions and lies, contained within the school text books, are able to earn a degree and serve as "obedient lackeys". They are among the most devoted servants of the capitalists, the billionaires.

That in no way changes the fact that the working people are "thirsting for knowledge", and believe that the University Professors can provide them with that knowledge. Who can blame them?

By the same token, the University Professors are well aware that it is in their best interests to perpetuate the same old myths, the lies of the capitalists. They have chosen to embrace a life of hypocrisy, in the service of the capitalists, and are reasonably well paid for this. To each his own.

Working people have got to learn, from their own experience, that the University Professors are in the service of the capitalists. They must be "knocked off their pedestal". This is *not* to say that we must wait until after the revolution, after we overthrow the capitalists, after we smash the existing state machine and establish the Dictatorship of the Proletariat. There is no need to wait. We can take action now. By proving that at least a few of their cherished theories are mistaken, we can help to empower the working class, to break the "invisible chains" of the University Professors, and at the same time, prepare the workers for the approaching revolution, and the subsequent Dictatorship of the Proletariat.

It may help to think of this as a "double play", or as "killing two birds with one stone", to put it in popular terms. After all, it is my belief that the most important thing now, the "key link", consists in preparing the working class for the Dictatorship of the Proletariat.

There are various aspects to this preparation. On the one hand, all workers have to be made aware of themselves as a class, with their own class interests, as opposed to the interests of the capitalists, the billionaires, the bourgeoisie. They also have to become aware of the necessity of smashing the existing state machine, and replacing it with a new, working class state apparatus, in the form of the Dictatorship of the Proletariat. The spiritual power of the University Professors, the invisible chains, is part of the existing state machine, and it has to be smashed. They must be exposed as the loyal servants of the capitalists, which they are.

We can manage this with the help of the most advanced members of the working class. Those who are most active in the class struggle can take part in proving the existence of various huge species, which the University Professors maintain are extinct. It is in this manner that the working people will realize that the University Professors are a pack of liars. The spiritual force, the invisible chains, the Professor Power, will thus be broken. At the same time, those same workers will gain valuable experience, training for the duties they will have to assume, after the revolution, under the Dictatorship of the Proletariat.

The reason I say this is because we are not anarchists -those who believe in no government- so that we have to face the fact that after the revolution, certain workers will have to be placed in key positions of authority. After all, it will then be necessary to crush the capitalists, as they try desperately to restore their "paradise lost". Of necessity, those workers will have to be among the most advanced members of the working class. Any training they receive now will prove to be most valuable.

As mentioned in a previous article, all University Professors maintain that basilosaurus, the "walking whale", is extinct. It most certainly is not extinct! In North America it is most commonly referred to as Ogopogo, and is located within many large lakes. It is also located in Europe, the most famous one being "Nessie", the Loch Ness Monster. My niece, who is Italian, tells me it is also in Italy. As these animals come out of the water to graze, after sun down, proving their existence should not be terribly difficult. The only thing required is an inexpensive, motion activated, trail camera. The working people taking part in this scientific break through, that of proving the existence of the "walking whale", will receive valuable training. There are other huge animals which must be proven to exist, in defiance of the University Professors. This can have no other effect than that of "knocking the University Professors off their pedestal", of "breaking the invisible chains", of overcoming the "spiritual force of repression", the Professor Power.

Although the University Professors will no doubt find this to be unpleasant, perhaps they can take some comfort in the fact that the alternative, that of being "tarred and feathered", as were their predecessors, is so much worse! Then again, at the time of the revolution, the working people will decide upon a course of action, focused upon their class enemies. All professional people would be well advised to bear this in mind. As yet, we have no idea of the precise form of that action. We just know that it will not be pleasant!

In the broadest sense of the term, this "Professor Power" can be extended to all people who have University degrees, and work in various fields, whether in government or industry. All are well aware that to ask "awkward question", is to "rock the boat", to risk "career suicide". This can result in being fired, and worse, being "black balled", so that they are never again allowed to work in their chosen field. That is power! Professor Power!

On a related matter, perhaps a little explanation is in order. I have my own personal religious beliefs, which I prefer to keep to myself. Properly so. I certainly have no quarrel with those who have other religious beliefs, and in particular, not with any clergy! It is important that all working people respect the beliefs of each other!

That stands in stark contrast to scientific theories, which are nothing more than scientific beliefs, and are meant to be challenged. Under no circumstances should this challenging of scientific theories be taken as a personal attack! Yet all too often, that is precisely the case.

As for the accusation that I have a prejudice against scientists, nothing can be further from the truth. In fact, I take inspiration from the pioneers of science, such as Kepler, Copernicus and Galileo. Those men risked their lives in challenging the "ecocentric" theory of the time, assuming that is the correct term. That was the belief that the earth was at the centre of the universe. If they had been caught, they would have been executed!

It was Newton who collected the work of those scientific pioneers and managed to put it all together. This resulted in his three laws of motion. As Newton put it, he merely "stood upon the shoulders of giants".

As a result of this, the "ice was broken", so to speak, and other scientists dared to speak up. In particular, Darwin bravely suggested the Theory of Evolution by Natural Selection. To this day, that has managed to rouse the wrath of numerous "fundamental" people, of various religious beliefs. They maintain that it fails to account for Creation!

To this I can once again respond that we should all respect those personal beliefs, including that of Creation. All working people have a common enemy, the capitalists, the billionaires. We have to overthrow the billionaires, and establish the Dictatorship of the Proletariat. The only way we can manage this is by putting aside our personal differences. We need a united front. The alternative is to continue life under capitalism.

Numerous other scientists were able to muster enough courage, despite some serious opposition, and were able to explain mysteries which had perplexed people. In particular, the existence of a great many huge animals, which must have lived many years ago, as was proven by the discovery of the fossilized remains of bones. This despite the fact that the bible failed to make any mention of those animals!

The problem was that at that time, by which I mean the time in which Darwin worked, it was thought that all the answers were located in the bible. There are a great many people who are still of that opinion. For my part, I respect those beliefs. But as perviously mentioned, I can only stress my opinion that our personal beliefs should be kept separate from the scientific theories.

So the scientists of that day, the earliest paleontologists, did the best they could and named these pre historic animals "dinosaurs". The choice of names was unfortunate, as it means "terrible lizard", and we now know that most of these animals were birds. That in no way changes the fact that the word "dinosaur" is now a house hold name. It is just one of those things with which we have to live.

Yet the scientific breakthrough had been made, and numerous others followed. The Egyptian Rosetta Stone was deciphered, and that made possible the translation of Egyptian hieroglyphs. In North America, Morgan was able to determine the social structure of primitive society.

That resolved the earliest mysteries of Roman and Greek civilizations. In South America, the ruins of various civilizations were discovered. Penicillin and various antibiotics were discovered. The transistor was invented. Let us not forget the aircraft and the internal combustion engine. All of these things, and many others, are commonly referred to as "progress".

So how is it that a great deal of scientific gobbledegook has found its way into the school text books? It clearly suggests that the "rot has set in", that we are making progress "in reverse", that "we are going backwards". And so we are!

The fact is that over the last few thousand years, numerous civilizations have come into existence, risen to a peak, prospered, and then fell into decline. They left behind the ruins, so as to remove all doubt!

Our civilization has also passed its peak, and is now in decline. That is not acceptable. Yet there is a difference between our civilization and all previous civilizations. Our civilization was the first to experience an industrial revolution. As a result of that revolution, two new classes were created, that of capitalists, bourgeoisie, and workers, proletarians. Now it is up to us, the working class, the proletariat, to reverse this decline. All previous civilizations could not prevent their own decline, because they did not have a progressive class of proletarians. We are the first civilization that is able to reverse our own decline! Now that calls for a little explanation.

The fact is that we live under a state of monopoly capitalism, referred to as imperialism. All imperialists have one thing in common: They are all reactionaries! There is nothing progressive about them. They care only about themselves. They are making every effort to drive our civilization into the ground, in the interests of making an ever greater profit. Further, they are performing a rather impressive job. They must be destroyed. That is where the proletariat comes into play!

This is not to say that the capitalists, the billionaires, are consciously determined to destroy our civilization. They are not. To suggest that is to give them too much credit. Nor are they trying to save our civilization. They simply do not care, one way or the other. The subject is a matter of complete indifference to them. They have given it no thought. They are focused on making a profit, becoming ever more wealthy, preferably a "Trillionaire"! Nothing else matters.

With that in mind, may I suggest that everyone face the fact that we live in a class society. As that is the case, either we serve the working class, the proletariat, or we serve the capitalist class, the billionaires, the bourgeoisie. There is no middle ground. Anyone who serves the capitalists, and that includes the University Professors and scientists, can and will find themselves a target of the revolution. Fair warning. That is just the way it is.

In fact, the professional people, whether Professors, scientists, engineers, teachers or administrators, have nothing to lose and everything to gain, by the revolution. Under capitalism, their jobs are never entirely secure. Regardless of how well they perform their jobs, they can be fired at any time, for any reason, or for no reason. The capitalists may choose to fire someone *because they can!*

By way of contrast, after the revolution, under the Dictatorship of the Proletariat, these professional people will play a key role in the new socialist society. They are currently serving the capitalists well. Soon, after the revolution, they will serve the working class just as well, probably much better. They will be treated with the respect they deserve, and paid quite handsomely. They will not have to commit to memory all the lies of the capitalists. They will not be subjected to the petty bickering and backstabbing, which is characteristic of all capitalist establishments. The work place atmosphere will be far more relaxed. Those who perform an exceptional job, can expect to be promoted.

Part of that job performance will involve training certain workers, those who are more advanced, in such technical work. The "cut throat" days of "every man for himself" has no place under socialism! Instead, the competition will be to perform to the highest standard. The factories, for example, which perform to the highest level, will serve as "model factories", in order to inspire the workers in other factories to perform just as well.

No doubt, there will be a period of adjustment, as people become accustomed to life under socialism. For the vast majority of people, this will be voluntary, as they embrace the improved conditions. Then again, for a significant minority, a certain amount of coercion will be required.

In particular, the monopoly capitalists, the billionaires, the bourgeoisie, will fight this "tooth and nail". This we can practically guarantee, as their standard of living will "nose dive". They will pine for the "good old days", when servants catered to their every whim, fleets of vehicles were at their disposal, clothes were worn once and thrown away, and a million or two was merely "loose change". The days of keeping a close eye on the stock market, of plotting and scheming to become the first "Trillionaire", will soon become a "dim and distant memory".

As no one wants to lower their standard of living, it should come as no surprise that the billionaires are no exception. They regard socialism, especially the Dictatorship of the Proletariat, as "hell on earth". After the revolution, we can expect them to go to any length to restore their "paradise lost". They will stoop to any depth, any level of deceit and deception. They will prey upon the weaknesses of the most honest. As they are superb liars, with life long experience, no doubt some working people will believe them. After all, there are so many people who believe that "there is a little good in everyone"!

That may or may not be true, and it may or may not be a fine philosophy. It matters not, as the class struggle calls for revolutionaries, not philosophers. We need tried and tested revolutionaries, hardened veterans of the class conflict, those without any illusions, to be entrusted with the task of crushing the capitalists, as well as their most devoted followers.

For that reason, it will perhaps be best to isolate the capitalists, or at least their leaders, in remote areas, depriving them of any means of communication. At the same time, we want everyone to be useful, so perhaps a job in underground mining is something they can handle.

There are other members of that small but significant minority, and they are referred to as class traitors. These people are members of the working class, yet at the same time, they are completely loyal to the capitalists. Under capitalism, for reasons which defy all rational explanation, these workers consistently "lick the boots" of the capitalists. They go out of their way to curry favour with the bosses, "ratting out" their fellow workers at every opportunity. The reward for such self degradation is -absolutely nothing!

Under socialism, we can expect these same boot lickers to defend the billionaires, to demand that we return to them all the wealth they have stolen. In that case, perhaps it would be best to allow these class traitors to accompany their Lords and Masters. They can join them in the mines!

As for those who remain skeptical, doubtful that anyone could possibly be that stupid, may I remind you that several servants accompanied Czar Nicholas and his family, after he was removed from the throne and placed under arrest. Those same idiots also died with Nicholas and his family. I mention this as an example of extreme stupidity, in conjunction with a spiritual force.

This is to drive home the point that there are various "spiritual forces of oppression", to use the expression of Marx, or "invisible chains", which is my expression. These are in addition to the "physical force elements", all part of the "existing state apparatus", once again according to Marx, all of which must be destroyed.

To destroy the physical is not terribly difficult. Brute force is required, and there is no shortage of working people who are experts in that department! Yet spiritual forces must also be destroyed, and brute force alone is not sufficient. The people who are in possession of these "spiritual forces of repression" must be crushed.

These spiritual forces are not to be underestimated. Just because they are invisible, does not mean that they do not exist! They merely supplement the physical force element, and if anything, are more dangerous. Because they are invisible, they are well hidden.

We must not repeat the mistakes of previous revolutionaries, but learn from them. At the time of the Chinese revolution, the spiritual power of the landlords, over the peasants, was broken. Yet the spiritual power of the University Professors, over all the common people, both peasants and workers, was not broken. This served to enable the Chinese capitalists to return to power.

At the time of the Second American Revolution, we can expect the spiritual power of the Mobsters to be broken, just as the spiritual power of the Tories was broken, by their ancestors, at the time of the First American Revolution. Yet the spiritual power, the University Power, of the professors will also have to be broken. Otherwise, we run the risk of a return to power, by the capitalists.

For now, may the revolutionary battle cry be:

Prepare For Council Power
and the Dictatorship of the Proletariat!

CHAPTER 9

Putin, A Typical Imperialist

Mar 8, 2022

On February 24, 2022, Russia invaded the neighbouring country of Ukraine. As the Russian military is far stronger than that of Ukraine, it was thought that the war would be over very quickly, with Ukraine under Russian rule. Such is hardly the case, as the Ukrainians have put up a heroic resistance. The whole world is watching closely, especially as the threat of nuclear war is paramount.

It is very likely that a great many people are confused, as they tend to identify Russia with the Soviet Union, the country which was able to absorb the assault of the Nazi invasion of 1941, the same Nazis which had conquered western Europe. The Soviet Union was then able to go on the offensive and defeat the Nazis. Of course, in the process, the sacrifices of the Soviet people were appalling.

So in the interests of providing a little clarification, a brief lesson in history is required.

We can start by facing the fact that on November 7, 1917, (new style calendar) the Russian revolution, led by Lenin, succeeded in establishing the first successful socialist republic in the world. The Russian empire was dissolved, so that the countries which had been ruled by Czarist Russia, were able to achieve independence. The country of Russia was declared to be a republic, which is to say that it no longer recognized any monarch, and the official name of the country became Soviet Russia.

As an aside, the word Soviet, in Russian, means Council, in English. I mention this as it is so important. The Russian revolutionary motion spontaneously gave rise to Soviets, or Councils, just as is happening now in North America. Just as these Soviets formed the basis of a new proletarian state power, after the revolution, we can expect the same thing here in North America. But to proceed.

After the socialist revolution, it was not "smooth sailing". The country was still at war with Germany, Austria-Hungary, Turkey and Bulgaria, referred to as the Quadruple Alliance. Russia was able to secure peace with those countries, but at a very high price. Each and every one of them wanted a "piece of Mother Russia", and they got it, in the Treaty of Brest Litovsk, signed in March of 1918.

At that time, the country of Russia, in which three quarters of the people were peasants, was in ruins. There followed a brief interlude of relative peace, in which Lenin and the Bolsheviks, as the Marxists of the day were then called, were able to make a start at rebuilding the country.

On November 11, 1918, the First World War was over. An Armistice was signed, and the imperialists of the various countries "came to their senses", so to speak. They realized that socialist Soviet Russia was a common enemy, and determined to destroy that country and Bolshevism, along with it. (At that time, the Communists were called Bolsheviks) With that in mind, the countries of Britain, France and America, were able to arm and equip numerous rebel armies, in countries adjacent to Russia. These troops were referred to as "Whites", as opposed to the Russian "Red" army. Their goal was to crush the upstart Soviet republic. They very nearly succeeded. At one point, three quarter of the country was occupied by the invading armies, and the Russian Soviets, the Red Army, were fighting the war on five fronts! Against all the odds, they succeeded in driving out the invaders. After all, they were fighting for their freedom, and were led by Lenin and the Bolsheviks. There are similarities to the situation that currently exists in Ukraine!

It was only in 1921, after three years of civil war, that the invaders were finally driven out. At that point, Russia was able to adopt a policy of modern industrialization, in order to prepare for the anticipated next invasion. After all, the imperialists are not about to allow a socialist state to live in peace!

This brings us to the subject of imperialism, of which so much has been written. No doubt many people are wondering how it differs from capitalism. Lenin explained this very well, in his excellent book, Imperialism, the Highest Stage of Capitalism. In fact, imperialism is nothing other than capitalism, in its highest stage, that of monopoly. This transition took place at or around the beginning of the twentieth century. Imperialism, or monopoly capitalism, is somewhat different from "free market capitalism". In fact, it has five essential features, as Lenin explained:

"1) The concentration of production and capital developed to such a stage that it creates monopolies which play a decisive role in economic life

"2) The merging of bank capital with industrial capital, and the creation, on the basis of 'finance capital', of a financial oligarchy

"3) The export of capital, which has become extremely important, as distinguished from the export of commodities

"4) The formation of international capitalist monopolies which share the world among themselves

"5) The territorial division of the whole world among the greatest capitalist powers is completed

"Imperialism is capitalism in that stage of development in which the domination of monopolies and finance capital has established itself; in which the export of capital has acquired pronounced importance; in which the division of the world among the international trusts has begun; in which the partition of all the territories of the globe among the great capitalist powers has been completed".

That is a rather complete definition of imperialism, rather technical, but very accurate. Yet the question remains, whether it is possible to reform imperialism? The answer is that, as Lenin stated: "the political features of imperialism are reaction all along the line, and increased national oppression, resulting from the oppression of the financial oligarchy and the elimination of free competition". In other words, most emphatically, no!

For the benefit of those readers who are something other than "Philadelphia lawyers", I will mention that the internet gives a rather fine definition of a reactionary: "In political science, an ultra conservative, a person who holds political views that favour a return to the status quo, the previous state of society, which that person believes possessed positive characteristics, absent from contemporary society".

As all imperialists are completely reactionary, it stands to reason that we can expect nothing progressive from them. Nor is there any point in trying to "turn back the hands of time", to the time of competitive capitalism, as it simply cannot be done. Now it is simply a matter of destroying the imperialists.

To return to Russia of 1921, which was in a state of complete ruin, after seven years of war, Lenin determined that the only way to industrialize the country, was to *invite in the foreign capitalists!* This gave birth to the New Economic Policy, in which the capitalists, of various countries, were able to invest their capital, make a huge profit, while converting Russia into a highly industrialized country. In fact, within twenty years, the country went from being "one hundred years behind America", to being almost on the same level.

Also, in 1922, the country of Russia united with several other socialist republics, which had formerly been crushed by the Czarist Russian Empire. These included the republics of Ukraine and of Belorussia, among others. This in turn gave birth to the socialist Soviet Union. At about the same time, the Bolsheviks, Marxists, adopted the name Communists.

Sadly, Lenin died in 1924, so that Stalin was forced to "carry the torch". The economic development that Lenin had started was carried forward, so that the country became highly industrialized. The Soviets managed to accomplish, in twenty years, that which it has taken the capitalists, one hundred years to manage! This did not happen any too soon, as of course, the Nazis first conquered western Europe, in 1939 and 1940, and then invaded the Soviet Union, in 1941.

It was only because of the leadership of Stalin and the Communists, as well as the fact that the country was highly industrialized, that the Soviets were able to repel the assault of the Nazis. Yet upon the death of Stalin in 1953, the Russian capitalists were able to return to power. They then promptly embraced imperialism!

For the next few years, the Soviet Union became known as the "chauvinist" Soviet Union, "socialists in words, chauvinists in deeds". Then it collapsed in 1989, so that the various republics were able to declare independence. Yet Belarus continues to have close ties with Russia.

In 2014, Russia invaded Ukraine, first captured and then annexed the Crimean Peninsula, in the southern part of the country. This has enabled Russia to attack Ukraine from the south, as well as the east, as Russia borders Ukraine to the east, and from the north, as Belarus borders Ukraine from the north.

Now ten days into the war, the journalists are questioning the "mental state" of Putin. They maintain that previously, he was "cold and calculating", but is now "erratic, unhinged, delusional, paranoid, terrifying, isolated, not listening to reason". In fact, he placed his nuclear forces on alert.

The western forces of NATO consider this to be a threat of nuclear war. For that reason, they are reluctant to declare a "No Fly Zone" over the country of Ukraine. Their fear is that it would almost certainly result in the downing of Russian aircraft, and the beginning of World War Three, a nuclear war. Their fears are well grounded.

This is not to say that Putin is a mad man, a raving lunatic. He is not. He is merely a typical imperialist, a complete reactionary, determined to return to the "good old days" of the Russian Empire. He is no different from any other imperialist, of any other imperialist country.

This is to say that the countries of NATO, the North Atlantic Treaty Organization, which includes the countries of North America and western Europe, are also imperialist. The leaders of those countries are every bit as reactionary as Putin!

It is clear that the war is not going the way Putin had planned. Not at all. For several days, a massive convoy of thousands of vehicles has been parked outside the capital city of Kiev, apparently out of fuel, food and spare parts. As well, the Ukranian air force has not been destroyed. The plan to capture Kiev and secure the country within several days, has proven to be wishful thinking. But then, that is typical imperialist logic.

The American military experts are of the opinion that time is on the side of Ukraine. Each day they hold out, allows them to evacuate ever more civilians, get their hands on ever more weapons, which are being supplied by various countries, and become proficient with those weapons. As well, a foreign volunteer legion is being created and trained, in Lviv, in the western part of the country. Many of these soldiers are familiar with the latest armaments, and are prepared to train others.

The American military experts are impressed by the "creative manner in which the Ukrainians are attacking columns", which is high praise, considering the source! Among other things, they are using drones, which have proven to be quite effective.

The whole country has been mobilized. Civilians are producing camoflage netting, to be used to screen various weapons. As well, so called "Molotov Cocktails", or petroleum bombs, glass bottles filled with gasoline and soap, are also being produced, in great volume. The soap allows the gasoline to jell, so that it can be thought of as a "poor mans napalm bomb". These are also being referred to as "Lviv Smoothies".

As for those who consider these to be primitive and ineffective, bear in mind that at the time of the American invasion of Viet Nam, the Vietnamese used dried bamboo as weapons. Primitive, but supremely effective. Countless American service men can testify to the effectiveness of such "primitive" weapons!

On two occasions, the leaders of both countries have met for talks. It is reported that they agreed to "safe corridors", with cease fires, to allow for evacuations of civilians, and to allow humanitarian aid to enter the country. The trains in Ukraine are running supremely well, so that over a million civilians have already left the country. That number is expected to rise dramatically, so that the people who remain in the country, men and women, will be able to focus on the war effort, without having to worry about the civilians. It is clear that a great many modern weapons are reaching the troops on the front line. Of course, the Ukrainians are not disclosing just how these weapons are being delivered.

All American military analysts are agreed that the Russian invaders have made a "rookie mistake", in that they have not severed the Ukrainian communications networks. The Americans learned in Viet Nam, that to have journalists broadcasting live, from the war zones, as the troops are fighting, is not a good idea. The people at home should not be made aware of the slaughter that is taking place! It tends to intensify the anti war movement! God forbid that citizens should learn the truth! That is the last thing the military wants to see! For that reason, the American journalists were not allowed to film the next war, in Afghanistan. So the military was able to wage war, in relative secrecy, for another twenty years.

Now the Russian military is going through that same "learning curve", to use one of their ridiculous expressions. Even though the Russian media is producing glowing reports, concerning the "special military operation" in Ukraine, the Russian members of the public are receiving videos, or emails, on their computers and cell phones, concerning the true state of war. Opposition to the war, by the Russian civilians, is becoming ever more intense, as is the government crack downs.

Even without those videos, the members of the Russian public are aware that something is terribly wrong. The value of the ruble is now around one cent, due to inflation. The ruble has dropped dramatically. No doubt all working people are feeling the pinch.

The bourgeois press is reporting that the Russian "Oligarchs" are also being "targeted". They are careful to avoid the use of class terms! In fact, these oligarchs are members of the Russian bourgeoisie, the "super rich", the monopoly capitalists, the multi billionaires. Various governments are seizing their yachts, private jets and luxury apartments. As it is assumed that they have political connections to Putin, it is thought that they will put pressure on Putin, to end the war. If nothing else, it is a happy thought.

The president of Ukraine, Zalensky, has been calling upon NATO to provide a "No Fly Zone" over Ukraine. Such a Zone would be to the advantage of Ukraine, as the Russians have a vast air superiority. So of course Putin is dead set against this.

Even the NATO military analysts are agreed that such a Zone could lead to a "broader war", even "World War 3", a "nuclear war", as it would lead to Russian aircraft being shot down, and Russia would consider that an act of war. Imagine that!

Yet there is a "back door", as the press refers to it. They are referring to the "United Nations Articles 27 and 52". The journalists say that those two articles give the United Nations -UN- the right to establish a No Fly Zone over Ukraine. They can do this with the "vote of nine members of the fifteen member UN Security Council". The press also reports that as Russia is "part of the conflict", it has to "abstain from voting".

This may or may not be true. The point is that the NATO imperialists are determined to take control of Ukraine, and they are quite prepared to risk war, even nuclear war, in the process.

Ever more NATO troops are being sent to western Europe. The French have just sent an aircraft carrier to the region. The Americans have sent huge B52 bombers to the area, within "one hundred kilometres" of the border.

It is clear that the western imperialists are squabbling with the Russian imperialists, over the "juicy little morsel" of Ukraine. It is the current "bone of contention". It is also clear that the people of Ukraine are putting up a heroic resistance, against the Russian invaders. Those people certainly deserve our complete support.

This is not to say that we should support the imperialists of the west, in the form of NATO, against the Russian imperialists. It is up to all working people of the world to unite, to oppose all imperialists, starting with the imperialists of our own countries.

It is also up to conscious people, those who are aware of the revolutionary theories of Marx and Lenin, Communists, to raise the level of awareness of working people. Of necessity, most of those people are current or former members of the middle class, the petty bourgeois. As best I can gather, that is not happening. At least, if it is happening, it is a well kept secret, and that defeats the purpose!

As I explained in a previous article, it is only in university that people are exposed to the revolutionary theories of Marx and Lenin, and then only with a view to distorting those theories. It is also a fact that such a university education is limited mainly to the bourgeois, the children of capitalists. The children of very few working class people are able to go to university.

Yet the "cultural level" of the working class, the proletariat, has increased dramatically, within the last few years. Countless working people now own computers, or various "digital devices", which include cell phones, smart phones and whatever else. These are now being used to take pictures and videos, and can be posted instantly onto the internet. They can also download from the internet. Precisely what we need!

As stated previously, the middle class intellectuals are not performing their duty, that of raising the level of awareness of the working class, the proletariat. So now it is up to the working class to educate itself. Yet now we have to go one step further, to literally unite with the workers of all other countries, through the internet. That includes the working class of Russia, as well as of Ukraine. The working classes of all the NATO countries must come together with the working classes of all the eastern countries. We must take to heart the slogan, suggested by Marx himself, that of: Workers of the World, Unite!

It is the combination of a high cultural level of the working classes, of so many countries of the world, along with the existence of the internet, which makes this possible. As well, the fact is that a great many working people are multi lingual, so that workers in one country can now communicate with workers of different countries, in their own languages. All can be encouraged to download the "Essential Works of Lenin", including State and Revolution, Imperialism, the Highest Stage of Capitalism, and What Is To Be Done? An understanding of those revolutionary works will provide a solid grounding in the theories of Marx and Lenin.

In addition, the workers of various countries can discuss, on the internet the anti war, anti capitalist movements, in their own countries. They can even coordinate their revolutionary activities. This will have the effect of strengthening the international working class revolutionary movement. Every capitalists worst nightmare!

In particular, the working class of Russia must be assured that they are our Comrades. We have the same class enemy.

Putin and the "Oligarchs", which is to say the members of the Russian class of bourgeoisie, are now the "new Romanovs", the "new nobility", now ruling Russia. The names and faces are different, but the method of rule is similar. They amount to the new Russian monarchy, the new Czars. Just as the Romanov's were overthrown, so too Putin and the Oligarchs will be overthrown.

Even though Lenin is no longer with us, his works are readily available. As a fellow Russian, he outlined precisely the manner in which the Czar had to be fought and then overthrown. His advice is as valid then, as it is now. Legal work must be combined with illegal work. The level of awareness of the working class must be raised. Use the internet to download works of Lenin and Marx. Send emails to as many working people as possible. Trust on one. No doubt Putin has agents working within the working class, informers who are more than happy to "rat out" a fellow worker.

Bear in mind that it was Lenin who first organized the League of Struggle For the Emancipation of the Working Class. He was also promptly thrown into prison. Try to avoid prison, as people who are locked up, are of limited usefulness.

With that in mind, those who are more familiar with the internet can put their training to good use. There must be a way to communicate with each other, without the government authorities becoming aware. The pedophiles and "human traffickers" do this on a regular basis. If they can do this, then we can do this.

The Russian people are supremely proud, with good reason. It is the country of Lenin, with a history of revolutions. It was Russia that demonstrated to the world the manner in which a most reactionary monarchy could be overthrown, and then the capitalists in their turn, and how to establish Soviet Power and the Dictatorship of the

Proletariat. Now the Russian working people will show the world how to restore the Dictatorship of the Proletariat.

We will know we are achieving our goal when protesters from Kiev to Moscow, from Washington to Beijing, carry banners which proclaim:

Workers of the World, Unite!

CHAPTER 10

Gun Control: Another Issue That Is Dividing the Working Class!

The press is reporting that "gun violence" in America is now at "epidemic proportions". So far this year alone, there have been over 230 incidents of "mass shootings". The year is less than half over!

Further, a "mass shooting" is defined as one in which four or more people are shot. Shootings in which less than four people are shot, are not documented! Everyone agrees that "something should be done"! Suggestions range from the ridiculous -teachers should be armed!- to the more ridiculous, that of banning all firearms!

President Biden has responded by "taking the bull by the horns", and televising a speech, during "prime time", no less. He wants to pass laws, restricting "assault weapons", such as the AR15, among other things. He even went so far as to say that during a previous ten year period, at which time those weapons were banned, the number of mass shootings had declined. This is a strong argument in favour of banning assault weapons. Too bad it is not true!

His critics have pointed out that Biden is doing that which he does best. He is stating "facts", which exist only in his imagination! The fact is that Americans have a "Bill of Rights" in the Constitution, referred to as the First Ten Amendments. The Second Amendment is as follows:

''A well regulated militia, being necessary to the security of a free state, the right of the people to keep and bear arms, shall not be infringed."

The fact of the matter is that the Constitution gives Americans the "right to bear arms", and this right shall "not be infringed"! Any laws concerning "gun control", may well "infringe" upon this right! Such a law is referred to as "unconstitutional"! That did not stop President Biden from proposing laws that would do just that! This is to say that he is proposing to violate the Constitution, the very Constitution that he swore to "preserve, protect and defend!"

This in turn gave rise to calls for impeachment! Yet cooler heads prevailed. They pointed to the fact that the "second in line to the presidency" is the Vice President, which is to say, Kamela Harris. Further, "number three" is the Speaker of the House, Nancy Pelosi.

To remove Biden from office, would automatically place Harris in the "Oval Office", and to remove Harris from office, would result in Pelosi becoming President! This was followed by references to Mo, Larry and Curly, of the Three Stooges fame. Yet the biggest fans of the Three Stooges said that that Joe, Kamela and Nancy, are not in the same league as the original Stooges. They are but a poor imitation!

Other wits among the working class have come up with another joke: "Pray for the health and well being of Joe Biden! Kamela Harris is a heart beat away from the presidency!" It may be objected that the slaughter of so many innocent Americans, including children, is not a joking matter. True! It is also a fact that this "gallows humour" is an indication of the level of bitterness, frustration and anger, of so many Americans.

One official has even suggested that the federal government should call out the National Guard! He thinks there is no other way to "restore law and order", at least to the city of Baltimore! The fact of the matter is that the country is close to a state of anarchy. Jungle law! Kill or be killed! Survival of the fittest! Every man for himself!

What is more, the "Authorities" do not know what to do! This amounts to a "crisis in capitalism", so that the ruling class must "change their method or rule". In this case, it is clear that the capitalists are considering a declaration of "Martial Law"! At that time, the military will be called in. The Constitution, along with all democratic rights, will be "null and void". The "Right to bear arms" will no longer be an issue! Americans will have no rights!

This is to say that the situation is revolutionary! The ruling class of capitalists, the bourgeoisie, can no longer rule "in the old way", and the "lower classes", the proletariat, find the current situation to be "intolerable".

Lenin had a few words to say about such a situation, in Left Wing Communism, An Infantile Disorder. This was written shortly after the successful Socialist October Russian Revolution of 1917. As it is so exceptionally important, I have chosen to quote it at length: "The fundamental law of revolution, which has been confirmed by all revolutions and especially by all three Russian revolutions of the twentieth century, is as follows: for a revolution to take place, it is not enough for the exploited and oppressed masses to realize the impossibility of living in the old way, and demand changes; for a revolution to take place it is essential that the exploiters should not be able to live and rule in the old way. It is only when the *"lower classes" do not want* to live in the old way and the *"upper classes" cannot carry on in the old way* that the revolution can triumph.

This truth can be expressed in other words: revolution is impossible without a nation wide crisis (affecting both the exploited and exploiters). It follows that, for a revolution to take place, it is essential, first, that a majority of workers (or at least a majority of the class conscious, thinking and politically active workers) should fully realize that revolution is necessary, and that they should be prepared to die for it; second, that the ruling classes should be going through a government crisis, which draws even the most backward masses into politics (symptomatic of any genuine revolution is a rapid, tenfold, and even hundredfold increase in the size of the working and oppressed masses -hitherto apathetic- who are capable of waging the political struggle), weakens the government, and makes it possible for the revolutionaries to rapidly overthrow it." (all italics and parentheses by Lenin)

I suspect that all readers, of all political persuasions can agree, that this is a very accurate description of our current state of affairs. Revolutionary! It is not just the shooting of innocent civilians, including school children! There is also sky rocketing inflation, fuel prices "through the roof", and a shortage of necessities, including baby formula! The capitalists have now stooped to the depths of starving our babies, by creating a shortage, so as to raise prices, thus increasing profits! Not to mention massive unemployment, homelessness, and the degradation of relying on food banks!

The list is endless!

Now the choice is crystal clear: Anarchy or Socialism! Further, just as I stated in an earlier article, the choice is up to you ladies! You ladies, and only you ladies, have demonstrated the ability to organize nation wide protests! Now is the time to put those skills to good use! No doubt, previous experience has taught you that such protests are of limited usefulness. Half measures get you nowhere! Capitalism must be abolished! The ruling class of capitalists, the bourgeoisie, must be overthrown! The current state apparatus, which has been set up to crush us, must be smashed! It must be replaced with a new state apparatus, in the form of the Dictatorship of the Proletariat!

There is no time to lose! Revolutions are not "made to order!" In fact, it could break out any day now! The level of tension in the country is severe! Now is *not* the time to organize protests! Now is the time to *organize an Insurrection!* As I have gone into this in other writings, there is no need to repeat it here.

I can only summarize that we need to combine the various Councils, raise the level of awareness of the proletariat, form a true Communist Party, Dictatorship of the Proletariat, and carry out an Insurrection. Such an Insurrection has a far greater chance of success, than one that is spontaneous. Which is not to say that an organized Insurrection has any "guarantee" of success! The only "guarantee" is that an unsuccessful Insurrection, will change nothing! Bear in mind that in Russia, in October of 1917, under far more difficult circumstances, a successful socialist Insurrection took place. May that be an inspiration for all of us.

CHAPTER 11

Prepare For Council Power and the Dictatorship of the Proletariat

The revolutionary motion is growing ever stronger. Even the journalists, including those who are the strongest supporters of the capitalists, admit that the country is "deeply divided", a "powder key", ready to explode. This is true.

As for those who are skeptical, thinking perhaps that a revolution could not possibly happen here, feel free to face the facts. Bear in mind that the interests of the two classes, the proletariat and the bourgeoisie, are diametrically opposed. The wealth of the capitalists comes at the expense of the workers. The more wealth the capitalists gather, the more impoverished the workers.

Yet according to the bourgeois economists, since the start of the pandemic, less than two years ago, the wealth of the billionaires has doubled! These same bourgeois economists also report that the billionaires pay little or no taxes. Among other tricks of the trade, they may have "no income". They may merely "borrow" money, from a company they own, as a means of supporting their lavish life style. Tax free!

There are numerous other ways to avoid paying taxes, all of which are perfectly legal!

There are now a number of billionaires who are worth tens, and even hundreds of billions.

It is not enough! Each and every one of them wants to be the first "Trillionaire"! In other words, they want to possess the wealth of a thousand billion!

As one of these multi billionaires explained, in response to the suggestion that he should pay his "fair share" of taxes: "Eventually, they run out of other peoples money, and then they come after yours". The billionaires see themselves as victims! Another billionaire stated it more prosaically, in response to the suggestion that he pay taxes, with a possible attempt to sound profound: "It is better to get humanity to Mars, and preserve the light of consciousness".

Rather than pay taxes, in order to provide housing for the homeless, medical care for those whom so desperately need it, food for the hungry, repairs to the infrastructure, such as roads and bridges, among a great many other things, he considers it more important to "preserve the light of consciousness" by "sending humanity to Mars"!

To think that the social chauvinists would have us believe that such people are about to "submit to the will of the majority"! Not likely! The point is that the situation is truly revolutionary, as there is a limit to that which working people are about to tolerate.

It is also true that this movement is beyond the control of "mere mortals". At some point it will break out into full scale revolution. We had best be prepared. An Insurrection which is well organized, has a far better chance of success, than one which is spontaneous.

The key word here is "prepare"! The most advanced workers must become class conscious, aware of the existence of classes. They must also become aware of the revolutionary theories of Marx and Lenin. The necessity of smashing the existing state machine, and replacing it with the Dictatorship of the Proletariat, must be stressed. They must also be trained. It is essential that they work together, as a team, in the class struggle, against the capitalists.

With that in mind, may I suggest that the search for certain animals, which the scientists insist are extinct, can be considered part of that training. The experience that working people are about to gain, in proving the existence of these huge animals, will prove to be most valuable.

As for those who dispute that statement, may I point out the fact that Lenin stressed the importance of *"all sided* political exposure. In *no other way* can the masses be trained in political consciousness and revolutionary activity . . . Working class consciousness cannot be genuinely political consciousness unless the workers are trained to respond to *all cases* of tyranny, oppression and abuse, no matter *what class* is affected". (italics by Lenin)

Here we have an example of the capitalists, using the scientists, to deprive the working class, of their heritage. The act of proving the existence of these animals, thus restoring their heritage, will dramatically increase their level of awareness, their "political consciousness".

Having said that, we can now consider the "Councils", a creation of the revolutionary movement.

These Council are composed of leaders of the working class, and such people plot a course of action for working people, usually within a particular neighbourhood.

In the city of Seattle, they actually set up a "Zone", and declared it to be "Autonomous". They very quickly learned, just as the workers who took part in the Occupy Movement learned, that such Zones are not allowed. The capitalists consider such Zones to be a threat to their authority, as indeed they are.

The Zone in Seattle, referred to as the Capitol Hill Autonomous Zone, was quickly crushed. Yet the Councils remain. May I suggest that these Councils assist in taking part in proving the existence of these huge animals, and in the process, train countless working people.

Incidentally, many people may not be aware of the fact that the word "Council", in Russian, is "Soviet".

These Councils, or Soviets, are spontaneous creations of the working class. They first appeared in Russia, in 1905, at the time of the first Russian revolution. As they eventually gave rise to the Soviet Union, they are not to be under estimated. It is not a coincidence that these Councils have also taken shape here, at this time. We too, are on the eve of a revolution. We have got to be prepared, and there is no time to waste.

May I suggest that working people first focus on the "myth" of Ogopogo", here in North America, or the "Loch Ness Monster" of Britain. Both "myths" are based on the same animal! They are not "myths" at all, but the basis of numerous legends. Yet the scientists insist that these animals do not exist!

That animal is basilosaurus. A whale. A whale with legs. A walking whale. A nocturnal walking whale. A predator, but not a carnivore. An omnivore.

This calls for a little explanation. To be nocturnal, is to avoid the light. This whale tends to spend most of the daylight hours inside caves. It also spends the winter months inside those caves. Then again, it is more likely to come out, if it smells blood. It is a predator, so that it eats flesh. Which is not to say that it is a carnivore, as it also eats vegetation. This whale is an omnivore.

After sun down, in the warm months, this whale comes out of the water, onto the meadows adjacent to the lakes, and grazes. It eats vegetation, mainly grass, no doubt.

I use the word "lakes", because this whale is widespread. There have been numerous reports of the animal being sighted, in a great many large lakes, at least here in North America. This is to say that the act of proving the existence of this animal, is simplicity itself.

There is no need for boats, complete with sonar, submersibles, and underwater cameras. Also no need of aircraft, with or without radar! The only thing required, is a simple, motion activated, trail camera!

With that in mind, may I suggest that some of these newly created Councils, especially those which are located close to large fresh water lakes, take steps to verify the existence of these walking whales. It is not difficult, but it is dangerous.

Perhaps teams of working people should be set up. Each team can be responsible for searching for meadows on one particular sector of a lake. Drones can be used for this. Once a suitable meadow is selected, then the trail cameras can be placed on trees, next to the meadow. One member of the team can be the "gun man", the one who carries a high powered rifle.

Other teams can be responsible for securing "eye witness accounts". This is a reference to those who claim to have "heard this animal". It is reasonable to assume, and numerous people have reported, that the animal makes "quite a racket" as it grazes!

These are very simple tasks, which could well be carried out by the scientists. They are not carrying them out, because the last thing they want to do is to "disturb the peace and tranquillity of the capitalists". That is the first thing we want to do! At the same time, workers will receive valuable training, and members of the Councils will get a chance to determine the suitability of those workers, to be placed in key positions, at the time of the Insurrection.

In particular, proof of the existence of walking whales will cause a major uproar. There will be an immediate call for the lakes, especially the Great Lakes, to be cleaned up. As they are severely polluted, mainly as a result of industrial run off, people will demand that the factories clean up their own mess. That is the last thing the capitalists want to hear! Perhaps if the politicians would spend less time squawking about climate change, and focus more on cleaning up our environment, then we would live in a far better world!

We can think of this as valuable training towards the Insurrection and the subsequent Dictatorship of the Proletariat, as that is precisely the case. After the revolution, after the capitalists are overthrown, and the existing state apparatus is smashed, certain workers will have to be placed in positions of authority, in order to crush the "desperate and determined" resistance of the capitalists, as they try to restore their "paradise lost". The training those workers receive now, will prove to be most valuable.

Working people are concerned with more than wages, living and working conditions. Mind you, those are important in their own right, and the gaining of such reforms are a by product of the revolutionary movement. In fact, such reforms tend to "strengthen and further the revolutionary motion". That is a fact. It is also a fact that the proof of the existence of various huge species, by the members of the working class, can also be viewed as a reform. After all, they are part of our heritage, a heritage which has been stolen from us, by the capitalists.

To restore our heritage, by the same members of the working class, will also have the effect of raising the morale of the working people. It will dramatically increase their self confidence, making them aware of themselves, as a member of a class of proletarians. It will also serve to "knock the scientists off their pedestals"!

At the same time, this will assist the members of the Councils, in their efforts to determine the suitability of certain workers for key positions, especially at the time of the Insurrection.

As I have documented in a previous article, on the day of the Insurrection, it will be necessary to shut down the railroads, bridges, tunnels, airports and sea ports, as well as communications networks. This is to say that all across the country, numerous groups of revolutionaries, working people, will have to take action, under the direction of a local Council. Each local Council, in turn, must work under the supervision of a national authority. We will go into that detail later, in this article. Each and every one of these groups must be resolute. If even one group fails to carry out its assignment, the fate of the Insurrection could be in jeopardy.

It is entirely possible that the revolution has already started! Recently, a major airline cancelled hundreds of flights, over a period of several days. The press reports are rather vague, but there are references to people who refused to work, including pilots and air traffic controllers. Assuming that such people are members of a union, then such "walkouts" are referred to as "wild cat strikes". This is a reference to a strike that has not been authorized by the union leaders.

If that is the case, then it is an indication of the strength of the revolutionary motion. Bear in mind that most revolutions start with strikes in the transportation industry. That includes railroads, airlines and shipping lines. As the capitalists are complaining about delays in shipping, it is entirely possible that the workers are engaging in "slowdowns". That is not exactly a strike, but very often a prelude to a strike. Such slowdowns take place as a result of deep worker dissatisfaction. As most union leaders are "in the pocket" of the capitalists, such dissatisfaction is completely understandable.

Strikes are one thing and Insurrection is something else entirely! At some point, the working people who are taking part in the revolution, have to seize political power! That calls for an Insurrection! That is not something to be taken lightly! The vast majority of the workers, or at least of the most advanced workers, must be prepared to overthrow the capitalists, smash the existing state apparatus, and establish the Dictatorship of the Proletariat.

A fine example of such a successful revolution, was that of October 25, old style calendar, or November 7, new style calendar, 1917, in Russia. It is commonly referred to as the "Great October Russian Revolution".

In fact, the revolution was not only successful, but also almost bloodless.

I mention the Russian revolution, as that is the revolution which most closely resembles our own.

Granted, there are considerable differences. In particular, the existence of the nobility, landlords and peasants, each with their own class interests, complicated that situation. Our situation is much simpler, in that we have the bourgeoisie and the proletariat. All other classes have been all but wiped out.

This is to say that we live in a highly industrialized, or "cultured" country, as opposed to an under developed, or "petty bourgeois" country. I mention this for the sake of those who are just now becoming politically active. It also means that starting a revolution in this country is much more difficult, as the bourgeois ideology is so deeply entrenched. Yet carrying the revolution through, after the Insurrection, is much easier.

Now to return to the Russian Revolution of October, 1917.

There is a reason that the revolution was not only successful, but also almost bloodless. It was well organized! At the time of the Insurrection, only the most determined, steadfast workers were placed in key positions. Those who tended to vacillate, or could even be expected to vacillate, were purged, removed from the Party, before the Insurrection.

This may sound harsh, but only because it is harsh. The time of the Insurrection is no time to be sentimental. It is the time to be completely audacious. Any weakness can prove to be fatal. The "defensive is the death of any Insurrection!", according to Marx! At such a time, the slogan must be, Victory or Death!

Just as in Russia, on the "Day of Reckoning", that of the Insurrection, various key locations, across the country, will have to be secured by the revolutionary proletariat. It is not enough to take possession of the "Vipers Nest", in the capital of Washington, D.C. Mind you, that little task will likely not be terribly difficult, as the events of January 6 have revealed. But then the capitalists have also noticed the weakness in their defences. So they have responded by building a wire fence around the buildings. Their childish faith in fences is somewhat touching, even if it is quite pathetic!

Bear in mind that in a similar situation, that of Russia in 1917, Lenin returned from exile in April, after the Tsar had been overthrown, and a "democratic republic" had been established, with the capitalists in charge. Yet Lenin did not immediately call for an Insurrection. In fact, a possible uprising in July of that year was aborted, as it was thought that the working class was not properly prepared. Those days have gone down in history as the "Revolutionary July Days".

I mention this because it is so important. Lenin called off a possible Insurrection, at that time, as it was clear to him that the working class, or at least the most advanced strata of the proletariat, had not fully embraced the Dictatorship of the Proletariat. This is another way of saying that the Russian proletariat was, at that time, not sufficiently class conscious. It was up to the Communists to raise the level of awareness, of the advanced workers, to that of the level of Communists. This they then managed, which in turn made possible the Insurrection, several months later, on October 25, old stye calendar, or November 7, new style calendar.

The American proletariat of today is even less class conscious than the Russian proletariat of 1917, through no fault of their own. The conditions of life, of the proletariat, do not lead to the awareness of itself, as a class. This awareness must be brought to it, from an outside source. That is the duty of middle class intellectuals. We clearly have our work cut out for us, but that is no reason for despair. Most working people are literate, and most of them have access to digital devices. The task of raising their level of consciousness is far easier for us, than it was for the Russian Communists of 1917.

Among other things, we have the internet, and we would be fools not to take advantage of it. It just means making popular literature available for the workers, very popular literature for the less advanced, but by no means vulgar. Feel free to use sports metaphors, and avoid the use of the word "backward", when referring to workers. So many workers may consider this to mean "stupid", and the last thing we want to do is offend any member of the working class. We want to flood social media with such literature.

No doubt, leaders will emerge. We would do well to bear in mind that working class people are avid readers. They pay strict attention to the news, so that in the literature, be sure to use current events.

No doubt, all members of the Councils are "Leftists", and consider themselves to be socialists, or are at least sympathetic to socialism. Equally without doubt, many of them are well aware of the revolutionary theories of Marx and Lenin. May I suggest that now is the time to apply those theories to a revolutionary situation. This is to say that a true Communist Party, one which calls for the Dictatorship of the Proletariat, is urgently needed. The creation of such a Party may not be terribly difficult.

I say that such a Party is "urgently needed", for good reason. Without a proper Party to organize the Insurrection, to coordinate the actions of the various Councils, throughout the country, then the Insurrection will be less likely to succeed.

This is *not* to say that the Insurrection is certain to succeed, under the leadership of a proper Communist Party. We can say that it is *far more likely to succeed!* We can also say that the Insurrection will almost certainly break out in the near future. If it fails, then rest assured, nothing will change!

Feel free to take inspiration from the workers of Paris, in 1871. At that time, an Insurrection was forced upon them. Against all the odds, they rose up and formed the "Paris Commune". As Marx put it, "they stormed the gates of heaven!"

Although brief, it was the first attempt of the Proletariat to seize political power, and provided Marx with valuable information. In particular, after the Paris Commune, Marx was able to stress the fact that the existing state apparatus must be smashed, and the workers must crush the capitalists, under the Dictatorship of the Proletariat.

May I suggest that the Communists, those whom are members of the various Councils, get in touch with each other. There is no need to meet in person. The idea is to form a proper Communist Party, one which calls for the Dictatorship of the Proletariat.

There are certain computer programs, which can be used for this purpose. Feel free to avoid certain words, as the government computers are programmed to "flag" such conversations. Do not make anything easy for the government agents! Bear in mind that as the pedophiles are able to use the internet, while escaping detection, so can we!

This is not to say that the Communist Party should take the place of the Councils. On the contrary, the Party should work as closely as possible with the Councils, especially in preparing for the Insurrection.

These Councils are a spontaneous creation of the working class revolutionary movement. They are also a proletarian form of state power! As yet, they are weak, but destined for great things! After the revolution, they will take part in the creation of a new government, under the Dictatorship of the Proletariat. They must be strengthened and encouraged!

The members of the working class, the proletariat, have created these Councils. That is as far as they can go! They are not aware of the revolutionary theories of Marx and Lenin!

For that reason, they cannot be expected to mount a proper Insurrection, smash the existing state apparatus, and establish the Dictatorship of the Proletariat!

This is to say that we need a proper Communist Party. Only such a Party can provide the proper direction. Only a true Communist Party can raise the level of awareness of the most advanced workers, to that of true Communists.

Half measures get us nowhere! Proper leadership is critical! The Insurrection could break out at any time! We had best be prepared!

The alternative is to continue to live under capitalism!

www.ingramcontent.com/pod-product-compliance
Lightning Source LLC
Chambersburg PA
CBHW032058020426
42335C300011B/392